EFFECTIVE LETTERS

LETTERS

A PROGRAM FOR SELF-INSTRUCTION

EFFECTIVE LETTERS

A PROGRAM FOR SELF-INSTRUCTION

second edition

JAMES M. REID, JR.
James M. Reid Company

ROBERT M. WENDLINGER
Assistant Vice President—Communications
Bank of America, San Francisco

with the assistance
and collaboration of
NEW YORK LIFE INSURANCE COMPANY

consultant
ROBERT L. SHURTER, PH.D.
Professor of English
Case Western Reserve University

McGRAW-HILL BOOK COMPANY

New York   St. Louis   San Francisco   Düsseldorf   Johannesburg
Kuala Lumpur   London   Mexico   Montreal   New Delhi
Panama   Rio de Janeiro   Singapore   Sydney   Toronto

234567890DODO79876543

This book was set in Journal Roman by Creative Book Services,
division of McGregor & Werner, Inc.
The editors were Richard F. Dojny, Harriet B. Malkin, and Claudia A. Hepburn;
the designer was Edward A. Butler;
and the production supervisor was Ted Agrillo.
The printer and binder was R. R. Donnelley & Sons Company.

Library of Congress Cataloging in Publication Data

Reid, James M
    Effective letters.

    First ed. prepared by the Programmed Instruction
Unit of the McGraw-Hill Training Materials and Infor-
mation Services Division.
    1. Commercial correspondence—Programmed instruc-
tion. I. Wendlinger, Robert M., joint author.
II. McGraw-Hill Book Company. Information and Training
Services Division. Effective letters. III. Title.
HF5721.R43 1973   651.7'5'077   72-7109
ISBN 0-07-051795-9
ISBN 0-07-051794-0 (pbk.)

CONTENTS

FOREWORD

As you may know, programmed instruction is an educational technique that relies largely on self-instruction.

Further, the teaming up of a publisher and an American business enterprise to coproduce the first full-length "programmed" course in effective letter writing represents an interesting cooperative venture.

The result, we hope, is a book that will help improve the way we communicate with one another in business, industry, and government. Hopefully, it should be useful to all who write, or expect to write, business letters.

Edward E. Booher, President
McGraw-Hill Book and
Education Services Group

Marshall P. Bissell, President
New York Life Insurance Company

PREFACE

In 1950, the New York Life Insurance Company introduced a continuing writing-improvement program, which many authorities have since called one of the best in the country. Manuals, bulletins, and films produced for the use of company employees are still requested and used by many college teachers, high school teachers, and libraries. These materials are also used in thousands of businesses, industrial firms, and government agencies.

In the early sixties, McGraw-Hill's Programmed Instruction Unit and New York Life Insurance Company's Public Relations Department used much of New York Life's original material to produce the first book to apply the then revolutionary technique of programmed instruction to the field of business-letter writing.

This second edition of *Effective Letters*, although basically the same as the first edition, has been reorganized, pruned, and expanded with new material and features. Specifically, we have rearranged it in three major parts, so that all chapters emphasizing editing and rewriting techniques (Chapters 1-14) will precede those chapters emphasizing the planning and writing of the whole letter (Chapters 15-18). Throughout, we have replaced various examples with fresher ones—taking particular care to provide a wider variety of types of letters, not only about insurance but about many kinds of business and governmental organizations. Chapter 18, "Persuade Your Reader," is all new and covers sales, collection, and application letters. We have also added eighteen chapter quizzes, located at the back of the book, to measure how well students have achieved each chapter's objectives. (Quiz answers are in the *Instructor's Manual*.) And, in response to frequent requests from instructors and students, we have provided an Appendix on letter mechanics and an Index.

ACKNOWLEDGMENTS

The second edition was again reviewed before publication by Robert L. Shurter, Ph.D., professor of English, Case Western Reserve University. Our thanks go to him for his many valuable comments and suggestions.

No less valuable have been the contributions of E. Van Fleet, Ed.D., assistant professor, University of Akron; Jack Yuen, Ed.D., professor, San Francisco State College; Madonna MacGowan, M.A., assistant professor, Adams State College (Colorado); and Judith Vaillant, associate director, Communications and Office Skills Training Institute, U.S. Civil Service Commission, who conducted field tests of the second edition manuscript in their business-writing classes. Their comments and reactions, along with the data obtained from student response sheets, have been of great help in making a final revision before publication.

James M. Reid, Jr.

Robert M. Wendlinger

INTRODUCTION

Please read this section before going on.

THE PROGRAMMED FORMAT

This book is different from a conventional textbook because it has a programmed-instruction format. That is, material is presented to you in small steps, called *frames*. Each frame gives you some information and then requires you to answer a question or practice a writing skill. After you have written your answer, you can uncover the correct answer and learn whether or not you were right. This whole process is much like having your own tutor. If you read carefully and want to learn, you probably will answer correctly most of the time, because preliminary drafts of this book have been tested on other students. Experience gained from these tryouts has helped to prevent your mistakes before they happen.

Because you are required to write answers to questions as you read, you may think of this programmed book as an exam or test. It is *not*, however, a test. It is a method of teaching which includes self-testing.

This programmed book is different in another way. It includes review and drilling exercises that an instructor using a conventional text would normally assign in the classroom. In a classroom, however, he can drill only one person at a time; the rest must wait their turn. But in this book you will be working continuously. Thus you will complete this course in *Effective Letters* in far less time than it would take if you were to use a conventional book, plus classes or meetings. Some programmed-instruction courses have cut learning time by as much as 50 percent.

You also benefit by working at your own speed. A programmed-instruction course does not require you to follow the pace of an "average" student. So choose a pace or tempo that suits you. We know that people learn at different rates but still may acquire the same amount of information. Each chapter should take about an hour to complete. If you take less time or more time, don't worry about it.

Now, a few words of advice:

1 Don't expect to spend an equal amount of time on each frame. Sometimes you will do a series of frames rather quickly and then come to a single frame that may take ten or fifteen minutes. Don't rush.

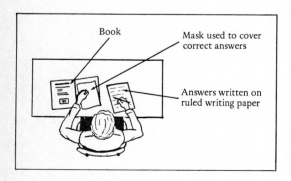

Book

Mask used to cover correct answers

Answers written on ruled writing paper

2 Misreading of frames often results in errors, so read very carefully before writing your answers.

3 When you do answer incorrectly, reread the frame. Don't go on to the next one until you understand why you were wrong. This is very important.

4 A programmed book, unlike a conventional book, cannot be scanned, crammed, or skipped. Nor should you begin to read in the middle of a chapter. Begin each chapter at the beginning, and don't stop until you come to the end.

5 You'll need some ruled paper on which to write your answers.

On the next page is a sample of the programmed instruction format that will appear in the following chapters. It will give you practice in using the format and an overview of exactly what we feel effective letter writing is all about. Please work through this sample and follow directions carefully.

Take the mask that has been inserted in this book and cover this page so that the top edge lies just beneath the arrow below. Then lower the mask slowly to the answer line. Do not go below the line until you have written your answer on your answer sheet.

Begin to study here.

> The difficulty is not to write,
> but to write what you mean,
> not to affect your reader,
> but to affect him precisely as you wish.
>
> Robert Louis Stevenson

1 Which of the following paragraphs best interprets Stevenson's words as they apply to business writing?_____

  A. A business letter will usually be effective because most business ideas are simple and easily communicated to a reader.
  B. It is traditional for business letters to use a special, impersonal language This language impresses readers and encourages a dignified and lasting business relationship.
  C. If a business letter is to be effective, its language must express the writer's meaning exactly. Moreover, the reader must react precisely as the writer wants.

Write the number of this frame (1) and the letter of your choice on your answer sheet. Then place your answer mask over the next page and draw it down to the next answer line.

Check your answer with this correct one.

 C (We think answer C is the best interpretation of Stevenson's words. Answer A just doesn't stand up, because many business letters must communicate complex and subtle ideas. For instance, business writers must often explain intricate points of company policy or procedures. A highly technical subject must be explained to a reader who is not well acquainted with the subject. Even a letter to Mrs. Doe explaining why her recent order was delayed requires careful thought and precise wording. Answer B is also not right. Any company can tell you about customers who were lost because its pompous, impersonal letters confused or insulted them.)

Using the same procedure, continue to study here.

THREE OBJECTIVES

All your business letters will have at least one of the following objectives:

To inform
To get action
To make a good impression

2 Which of the two sentences below has primarily the objective of *informing the reader?* _____

  A. Please sign the enclosed form and mail it to this office.
  B. You will receive $57.45 to pay your travel expenses.

  B

3 Which of these sentences has the primary objective of getting the reader to *do* something? _____

  A. Please telephone me on Thursday and I'll send over a messenger.
  B. Thank you for your thoughtful letter.
  C. Several of your fine recommendations have been adopted by management.

  A

4 Which of the following sentences is designed primarily to achieve the objective of creating a good impression? _____

  A. The meeting was held as scheduled on Thursday, June 2.
  B. Be sure to see the Tic Toc Koffee Maker at your local dealer.
  C. Mr. Saddler, who visited your plant last month, asked me to thank you for the pleasant tour you gave him.

  C

5 Below are three letters illustrating the three objectives. Write the letters *A, B,* and *C* on your answer sheet. Then write the words *to inform* next to the letter whose primary purpose is to inform the reader. Then write the words *to get action* by the letter which not only informs but asks the reader *to do* something. Finally, write the words *to make a good impression* by the letter whose sole purpose is to do precisely that.

  A. Dear Mrs. Hawley:

  I'm happy to tell you that your request for a building permit has been approved by the Zoning Board. We will mail it to you as soon as we receive the enclosed forms. Please fill them in, sign, and return to Mr. Conrad at our Bethel office.

B. Dear Mr. Gorman:

I have sent your cost estimates for the Newton construction project to our accountants for evaluation. I should have their reaction within a few days and will inform you of our decision no later than July 15.

C. Dear Miss Mathews:

Thanks so much for your nice letter about our skin products. It is good to know that we have such friends as you.

A. To get action (It also informs.)
B. To inform
C. To make a good impression

6a Now look at this short letter:

Dear Mr. White:

Thanks for sending me the pencil sketches for the cover of our July issue. I appreciate receiving them before the deadline. I'll telephone you about them on April 6.

This letter has two objectives. Which ones?_____

A. To inform
B. To get action
C. To make a good impression

A and C

6b Do you feel the above letter accomplishes its objectives?_____

Yes (We think so.)

7 Examine this letter:

Dear Mr. Grantham:

Your check finally arrived. It was for $15.63 instead of the $16.53 you agreed to pay. Obviously we cannot accept this check. We're returning it. Please send payment for the correct amount at once.

Do you feel that the above is an effective letter? _____

No (This letter does accomplish the objective of informing the reader of his mistake. It may also get the desired action, although we feel Mr. Grantham would be perfectly justified in sending a letter of complaint to the writer's organization. The above letter is rude and definitely does not make a good impression. It is not an effective letter.)

8a Which of the following two statements do you think is more accurate?_____

A. The effective business letter always tries to make a good impression on the reader.
B. An effective business letter usually tries to make a good impression, but sometimes this is not an objective.

B (Answer B is right. Some letters don't bother to make a good impression. A lawyer writing to notify someone that he's about to be sued, or a collection agent writing for the fifth time to someone whose bill is overdue probably would not worry about preserving goodwill.)

8b Do you feel that your business letters should try to make a good impression?

Yes (Most people write to associates, to customers, and to potential customers. If you do, their good opinion can help you and your organization in the years to come.)

9 Which of these statements, do you think, is more nearly true? _____

A. The objective of making a good impression is important but not as important as informing the reader or getting him to act.

B. Informing the reader, getting him to act, and making a good impression are all equally important objectives of a business letter.

B (All three objectives are equally important. Granted, the objective of making a good impression is most often neglected in business writing, and it's true that many letter writers don't take the trouble to even consider what their readers think of their letters, but this does not make it a less important objective.)

THE IMPORTANCE OF ACHIEVING OBJECTIVES

10 There's a very practical reason why your letters should achieve their objectives. Letters are a major business expense. Business and industry spend billions every year on letters.

No firm wants to waste its investment or even add to it by sending letters that do not inform and do not get the action they should. Unclear or unpersuasive letters represent wasted time and effort. They often require follow-ups which are an additional strain on the communications budget.

Nor do firms want to send letters that fail to make a good impression. Such letters waste their powerful potential to build goodwill. Since letters must be answered anyway, why not get the best return possible for your communications dollar? A good letter costs no more than a bad one. Usually it costs less.

Here are two versions of the same letter that were written by a custom shirtmaker to a customer who had returned his order of five shirts and complained that the collars were too large. Which do you think is more expensive? _____

A. Dear Mr. Wills:

Your shirts are being returned because obviously you don't realize that these collars are large on purpose. Normal shrinkage should result in a satisfactory condition. If we may be of further service, contact us at your earliest convenience.

B. Dear Mr. Wills:

Don't worry about the collar size of your shirts. We purposely make them two sizes too large to allow for normal shrinkage. After three or four washings, your collars should fit perfectly.

I am returning your shirts with this letter. If, after several washings, your collars are still too large, by all means send them to us and we will be most happy to replace the shirts without charge.

A [Letter A above is probably the more expensive. Notice the first sentence: "Your shirts are being returned because *obviously you don't realize* that these collars are large on purpose." "Obviously you don't realize" implies that the reader is at fault for not knowing about shrinkage. .

Notice the second sentence: "*Normal* shrinkage should result in a satisfactory condition." But what is normal? This sentence doesn't give enough information. Suppose, after a single washing, the reader again found the collars too large. He might return the shirts again and the whole routine would be repeated.

And the third sentence: "If we may be of *further service*, contact us at your earliest convenience." The phrase "further service" is highly inappropriate since the reader probably feels that the company has not been of any service to begin with.

Very likely, letter A would cost about $3.50 (the average price of such letters) *plus* the loss of a customer *plus* the loss of those friends who listened to his tale of woe. Letter B, however, courteously and clearly gives Mr. Wills the necessary information. If the shirtmaker had sent it instead of letter A, he probably would not have heard again from his reader, except to handle his renewed order for shirts.]

11   Most writers of business letters recognize the importance of informing the reader and of obtaining desired action from him because the achievement of these purposes is essential to the proper conduct of a firm's business. Fewer understand the need for creating a good impression. But by building goodwill with letters that make a good impression, you can distinguish your company from your competition and create a public relations climate that will help to clinch sales.

Put yourself in the reader's place for a moment. Suppose a reader, a financial analyst, is writing a report on the oil industry. He writes to two oil companies asking for copies of their financial reports. He also asks them about their methods of transporting crude oil. Here are the letters he receives.

Vaporex Oil Corporation

A. Dear Mr. Finley:

As you asked, I've enclosed our financial statement for the fiscal year ending June 30.

Your question about our method of transporting crude oil is a good one. Unlike most oil companies, we do not own a fleet of tankers. Rather, we rely on a subcontractor, the Manly fleet, which brings crude oil from our oil fields in South America to our refineries in Texas. This arrangement is simple and saves money.

Thank you for your interest in Vaporex Oil. I hope this information will help you write a favorable report.

Recon Oil, Incorporated

B. Dear Mr. Finley:

Enclosed you will herewith find the Recon Oil financial statement.

Regarding the question concerning the transportation of crude oil, Recon Oil makes use of its own fleet of tankers, which are sufficient to meet the requirements of crude oil transportation.

If there is a need for further service, do not hesitate to write Recon Oil, Inc.

Now suppose reader Finley is driving home from work and needs gas. He see two service stations on opposite corners. Which one is he more likely to drive into? That of Vaporex or that of Recon? _____

---

that of Vaporex (We think that all else being equal, most of the Mr. Finleys of this world would drive into the Vaporex station because they received a well-written letter which made a good impression.)

ANOTHER REASON WHY YOUR LETTERS SHOULD ACHIEVE THEIR OBJECTIVES

Effective letters are important to you too, as a writer. For if you spend a large part of your working day writing letters, you're a professional writer. Many business writers turn out more copy in a day than a working newspaperman, and as a business writer, you should want to do your job as professionally as you can. This means you should want to write effective letters.

Professional craftsmen know how to use the basic tools of their trade. If you are to become a craftsman of effective business letters, you must take the time to learn and practice the basic techniques and principles of effective letter writing. If you do, something like the following may happen to you.

Mr. Johnson, an insurance company employee, wrote the letter on page 10 to Mr. Green. A few days later Mr. Johnson received his own letter back, along with Mr. Green's check—with a note hastily scribbled on the bottom.

NEW YORK LIFE INSURANCE COMPANY   51 MADISON AVENUE, NEW YORK, NEW YORK 10010

September 2,

Mr. John R. Green
404 Main Street
Belleville, New York 13611

Dear Mr. Green:

This is a friendly reminder that your mortgage payment which was due on July 26 has not yet reached us. The August 26 payment is also due.

Everyone is apt to overlook things now and then, and if it has slipped your mind, please let us have your payment by return mail.

If payment has been mailed, please accept our thanks and disregard this notice.

Sincerely,

George W Johnson

George W. Johnson
Real Estate and Mortgage Loan
Department

Gentlemen: I am embarrassed – I did overlook payment. I was once a financial officer of a large corporation where I had to write collection letters. I struggled in trying to be friendly and effective at the same time! Your letter is the best I have ever seen.

Sincerely,
J. R. Green

Mr. Johnson showed this letter to his boss, who was impressed.

But who would care to have his boss receive the letter on page 11 from an important customer?

MERRYMOUNT TOYS, INC.
The Merrymount Building, Los Altos, California 94022

May 11,

Mr. Farley Auchincloss
President
Uniflex Steel Corporation
511 Daly Street
Scranton, Pa.

Dear Mr. Auchincloss:

I believe you will be interested in knowing the impression made upon me by the enclosed letter of reprimand from one of your company correspondents, James Mulreedy.

This condescending letter extremely annoyed me for many reasons. I am an adult and expect to be so treated by responsible companies with whom I do business.

I have been a customer of your company for a number of years, and it seems to me that your people could have treated the first oversight in this period in the payment of a bill in a more personal way. A well-worded letter, calling the fact to my attention, would have been understood. I believe our relationship should be a mutual one, with definite obligations, including courtesy, on each side. I do not believe that either you or I would be interested in buying something from a company which dealt with its good customers in the fashion represented by the enclosed letter.

I am not presuming to tell you how to run your business, but I do know from my own personal experience that courteous service goes a long way toward getting customers and keeping their business and goodwill. May I have your opinion on this?

Very truly yours,

H T Feeley

Harold T. Feeley
President

Let's summarize, then, with four reasons why effective letters are important.

1 They carry on the business of the organization by informing the reader and getting him to do what is necessary to the organization's progress.
2 Letters are a major expense, and this investment should not be wasted. A good letter costs no more than a poor one and usually costs less.
3 When a letter makes a good impression on the reader, it can help to influence public opinion and create a favorable sales climate.
4 You can help yourself professionally by writing effective letters.

THE EIGHT QUALITIES OF AN EFFECTIVE LETTER

All right, we've now covered why effective business letters are important. Now let's talk about the qualities of an effective letter. If your letters are to be effective, they should be—

    Clear
    Concise
    Forceful
    Well organized
    Natural
    Friendly
    Courteous
    Personal

We feel that business letters having the first four of the above qualities are *easy to understand* and those containing the second four have *proper tone.*

Clarity

Let's talk briefly about each of these eight qualities, starting with *clarity*. In order to have such a quality, a letter must be understandable without requiring several readings. Consider the following letter from an insurance company to a farmer:

Mr. Henry Blane
RFD 1
Brandywine, West Virginia 26802

Dear. Mr. Blane:

Surrender of the policy is permissible only within the days attendant the grace period on compliance with the citation relevant options accruing to the policy so we estopped from acquiescing to a surrender prior to the policy's anniversary date.

                                        Yours truly,

    Presumably the writer of the above letter had ideas he wanted to get across, but this letter was nonsense to the farmer, as it would be to most people who are not in the insurance business. To be effective, it must be understood by the person for whom it is intended—be he a carpenter, accountant, atomic physicist, or farmer. You must choose your words so that the reader will be sure to understand them without waste of time and effort.

Here is a classic example of another communication breakdown of this kind:

> A plumber found hydrochloric acid excellent for cleaning drains. He wrote a Washington bureau to find out if it was harmless. Washington replied as follows:

> The efficacy of hydrochloric acid is indisputable, but the chlorine residue is incompatible with metallic permanence.

> The plumber wrote back, thanked the bureau, and said he was very glad they *agreed* that it was effective. Back came:

> We cannot assume responsibility for the production of toxic and noxious residues from hydrochloric acid, and we suggest, therefore, that some alternative procedure be instituted.

> The plumber answered that he was getting fine results thus far. Would the bureau like to suggest the use of hydrochloric acid to other people? Finally, someone in Washington wrote:

> Don't use hydrochloric acid. It eats hell out of the pipes.

Although the third message is blunt, it is far superior to the others because the reader can understand it. Clarity, then, is the first requirement of an effective letter.

12 Which of the two sentences below is *clearer?*_____

A. He did not refuse to send the proper amount because he was not informed of the requirements.
B. Because he was not informed of the requirements, he refused to send the proper amount.

B

Conciseness

13 *Conciseness* is saying everything you have to say in the fewest possible words. This means be brief but *complete*. Dickens' *David Copperfield* has many thousands of words, yet for a hundred years, few readers have thought it was not concise. Nor have they thought that the *Gettysburg Address* (268 words) was too brief. Both works are concise because their writers said everything that had to be said in the fewest possible words.

This holds true in business writing as well, for a ten-page letter may be too brief and a one-page letter with a single paragraph may be wordy.

If you cut words from a sentence and that sentence loses either clarity or courtesy, then it is not concise but merely brief. However, you will *always* make a sentence more effective if you cut words and the sentence *doesn't* lose clarity and courtesy.

In the following three sentences, the writer wanted to say something and also make a good impression. Which sentence is concise?_____

A. During the past two weeks, we have been wondering if you have as yet found yourself in a position to give an indication of whether you have been able to come to a decision on our offer. (thirty-seven words)

B.   What about our offer? (four words)

C.   Could you tell us if you have decided on our offer? (eleven words)

C (Notice that sentence A is much too wordy. "During the past two weeks, we have been wondering" is unnecessary. The rest of the sentence is loaded with other unnecessary or wordy phrases. Sentence B is too abrupt, too brief. Some readers might very well react to this sentence with, "Well, what *about* your offer?" Sentence C is courteous and clear without being wordy.)

14   Someone has said,

"The writer does most who gives his reader the most knowledge and takes from him the least time."

However, many business writers believe that concise letters are abrupt or discourteous. But concise letters *include* courteous words, and conciseness itself is a form of courtesy. By packing more meaning into fewer words, you are clearer and more forceful. And you show courtesy to your reader by saving his time.

With competition for the reader's attention becoming keener every day, business writers must write concise letters. Your reader wants to know as quickly as possible what you have to say to him. He needs quickly understood, easily absorbed sentences.

Which sentence below is more *concise*? _____

A.   Today, business needs qualified correspondents.

B.   There is a need in today's business world for properly qualified correspondents.

A

15a   Which of the two sentences below is *clearer*? _____

A.   It is the understanding of those at this office that the shipment in the amount of four hundred steel girders has no situs in any of the states on the Eastern seaboard.

B.   We believe that the missing shipment of four hundred steel girders is not located in any of the East Coast states.

B

15b   Which sentence is more *concise*? _____

B

15c   The concise sentence is shorter by how many words? _____

Eleven

Force

16   Easily understandable writing is not only clear and concise but also *forceful*.

Force is a general term we use to sum up more concrete qualities. But for the moment, think of forceful writing as being *specific* and having *action.*

Weak: We seemed to be beset by a period of inclement weather.
Forceful: It rained every day for a week.

Notice that the first sentence contains many more general words than the second. Also compare the action verb "rained" with the vague and limp "seemed."

No doubt you have read a letter which you knew had something very interesting to say. Yet despite the inherent of its ideas, it bored you to death. The writer talked all around his subject, never coming to the point.

On the other hand, some letters capture and hold your interest even though the subject matter is rather ordinary. Your eyes jump from one sentence to the next, the writer's ideas developing clearly in your mind. This kind of writing interests you partly because it contains plenty of action verbs and specific words. It has *force.*

Read the following two paragraphs. Which is more forceful? _____

A. Minton engineers found that the redesigned Suprex Automatic Envelope Folder produces four hundred envelopes per minute. The machine's efficient cutter arm, which slices over an arc of only ¼ inch, increases its production by one hundred envelopes per minute. After thirty Folders were installed on the production line, total output shot up by 40 percent.
B. It has been concluded upon investigation by the Minton engineers that the redesigned Suprex Automatic Envelope Folder has a production rate of four hundred envelopes per minute. This represents an increased production capacity for the machine of one hundred envelopes per minute. The reason for this increase is due to a more efficient cutter arm which has a slicing arc of only ¼ inch. Installation of thirty of these devices on the production line has accomplished an increase of production of 40 percent.

A (The first paragraph is not only more concise than the second but more forceful and therefore more interesting to read. Perhaps you noticed that strong verbs such as "increases," "slices," and "shot up" are primarily responsible for making this paragraph forceful, while word groups such as "It has been concluded upon," and "the reason . . . is . . ." make the second roundabout and weak. The difference between these two paragraphs may not seem impressive to you at first glance, but, as you will see later, it is the difference between fair writing and effective writing.)

17a   Which of the following two sentences is more *forceful*? _____

A. Interviewing a carefully selected population has been the traditional method of doing market research by the Greg & MacDonald advertising agency.
B. The Greg & MacDonald advertising agency traditionally does its market research by interviewing a carefully selected population.

B

17b Which sentence has the more specific, more active predicate? _____

B (The predicate of sentence A is the *being verb* "has been," while the predicate of sentence B is the *action verb* "does.")

Good Organization

18 Writing that is easily understood is not only clear, concise, and forceful—it is also *well organized*. Sometimes, the difference between good and bad organization lies in putting ideas in their proper order. Examine the two sentences below. Which is better organized? _____

   A. To mix, place beaters in the revolving head of the electric mixer. Turn switch to "on."
   B. To mix, turn switch to "on." But be sure to place beaters in the revolving head of the electric mixer beforehand.

A (In A, the writer has properly instructed the reader to insert the beaters before turning on the mixer. In B, the instruction comes as an afterthought.)

19 When your letter contains relevant ideas only, when the major and minor ideas are clearly indicated, when these ideas are presented in the proper order, your letter is well organized. Examine the following. Which is well organized? _____

   A. A charge account is a convenience. For instance, if you want a book from our book department, simply call the store, ask for our book department, tell them what book you want, and say "charge it." Just sign and mail the enclosed card. Also, this privilege is available in all fifty-one departments of the store.
   B. A charge account is a convenience. For instance, if you want a book, simply call our book department and say "charge it." This privilege is available throughout our fifty-one departments. If you want to open an account with us, just sign and mail the enclosed card.

B (The first sentence of the sloppy presentation has so many ideas that the process of acquiring a book does not seem "simple" at all. The third sentence is out of place. It should have some sort of transitional phrase in front of it and should conclude the paragraph. In the well-organized presentation, only relevant ideas are included; they are given their proper importance and are presented in a clear, meaningful order.)

20 Which of the following two letters is better organized? _____

   A. Dear Mr. Danvers:

      I recently purchased some used office furniture and equipment at a bankruptcy auction held last Wednesday at a warehouse on Tremont Avenue. In the lot I purchased was an old Underwood typewriter. As you probably know, these machines are pretty good if they are fixed up, and it appears that this one needs some work. It looks like it has been stored in someone's attic and probably needs a good cleaning.

By the way, my secretary took a look at it this morning and says the ribbon does not wind properly. How long do you think it would take to fix it? I am writing to several repair shops to get estimates for this job. So I'd appreciate a prompt reply.

B.   Dear Mr. Danvers:

I would like to have your estimate for cleaning an old Underwood type-writer and for repairing the ribbon rewind mechanism.

May I have your estimate as soon as possible for the cost of the work and for the time it will take to complete the job? Thank you.

B (Letter A is very badly organized because it has a whole flock of ideas which are of no interest to the reader. Letter B gets to the point right away. It is well organized.)

Proper Tone

21a Now look at this letter:

Mr. Sam T. Muldoon
Langtry, Texas 78871

Dear Mr. Muldoon:

Your application for employment finally arrived last Wednesday. After care-fully examining it, I find that you are over sixty years old. This is much too old. So I am obliged to inform you that we cannot hire you at this time.

Sincerely yours,

This letter is easily understandable in that it is clear, concise, forceful, and well organized. But it is not effective, because it lacks the four qualities that are neces-sary to proper tone. In fact it is downright insulting.

Which of the two letters below has proper tone? _____

A.   I'm sorry that we no longer manufacture the Variflex model S-2 camera. Last June, we replaced the S-2 with our S-3 model, which has several new features. I am enclosing a pamphlet describing the new model. If you'd like to order one, we'll be most happy to hear from you. On the other hand, if you want an S-2, you might write to Sam's Used Camera Exchange, 802 Main Street, Flushing, New York. He ordinarily has a good supply of used models.

B.   We no longer find it worthwhile to manufacture the Variflex model S-2, as there is no demand for it. You may not be aware that as of June, 1972, the S-2 was replaced by the S-3, which is a far superior instrument. Enclosed herewith is a pamphlet describing the S-3 and an order blank. However, if you still want the old model, write to Sam's Used Camera Exchange, 802 Main Street, Flushing, New York.

A

21b What sort of person wrote Letter A? _____ (*Answer in your own words.*)

Your opinion, of course. But most people would think of him as courteous, friendly, and natural—in short, an intelligent, helpful fellow.

Naturalness

22 Many words can be used to describe a letter with proper tone, but we will stick to the four we listed earlier. Let's first talk about being *natural*. Effective letters are natural in that their wording is familiar to and comfortable for the reader.

If your words and phrases are pompous, unnecessarily technical, or old-fashioned, the reader will be distracted from your message. He will have to struggle with your phrasing before he can approach your ideas. He may think you are showing off your vocabulary rather than telling him what he needs to know. Or, he may even think you have no ideas at all.

Generally, the language of conversation is the best language for effective letters. It does not distract your reader but encourages him to concentrate on what you have to say. It is *natural*. Which of the following is more natural? _____

A. Its operational deficiencies were attributed by the agency to a lack of personnel resulting from budget limitations.
B. The agency said that it could not do a good job because it did not have enough money to hire enough people.

B (Notice how the long, overly complicated wording of sentence A calls attention to itself. As a reader, you must fight through this fog of big words to find the writer's meaning. Sentence B is easy to read because it is written in simple, conversational language that does not stand between the reader and the idea expressed.)

23 Which of the following sentences is more *natural*? _____

A. In the event that this does not meet with your approval, please notify this writer as to your wishes.
B. If you do not approve of this, please let me know what you want.

B

Friendliness

24 Proper tone also means that your letters should be *friendly*. These days, many readers are particularly sensitive to any suggestion that an organization, particularly a large one, does not care about individuals or is using its power unfairly. That is why it is important that your letters be as sympathetic, helpful, and concerned with the reader's problems as you can make them. Note the difference in the following two sentences. Which one is friendly? _____

    A. We are obliged to inform you that the completion of processing of your application has been delayed until the end of next week.

    B. I'm sorry that we've kept you waiting, but it's taken us a little more time than we expected to process your application. We'll have it completed by next Friday.

    B

25 Which of the following sentences are *friendly*? _____ (More than one choice may be correct.)

    A. Because you forgot to sign your employment application, I am returning it so that this oversight may be corrected.

    B. If you will send us a check for $159.61, we will be happy to ship your recent order for automotive parts right away.

    C. You must realize that we are doing everything in our power to investigate your claim that you did not receive our check for $1,000.

    D. As you asked, I am enclosing our annual report for the fiscal year ending December 31. Good luck with your report on the paper industry.

    B and D

Courtesy

26 If you use polite words like "please" and "thank you," and if you take the reader's point of view by recognizing his needs, your letters will be *courteous*. Which of the following is more courteous? _____

    A. May we please have your check for $23.97 by December 1?

    B. Submit your check for $23.97 not later than December 1.

    A

27 Which of the sentences below are courteous? _____

    A. May I visit you sometime during the week of April 28?

    B. Please accept my apologies for not answering your letter sooner.

    C. A prompt reply would be very convenient for me.

    D. If you had read the directions on the box carefully, you would not have broken the antenna while unpacking your radio.

    A and B

Personal

28 Finally, an effective letter will show the reader that you think of him not as a statistic but as a person. And it will prove that you are a person too, and not a mere cog in the organizational machinery. You can do both these things by getting *people* into your letters, by making your letters *personal*. Which of the following is more personal? _____

    A. It is hoped that the difficulties of the past two weeks have been overcome.

    B. I hope that you have overcome your difficulties of the past two weeks.

B (Notice that in sentence A all mention of the reader—or the writer—has been carefully avoided. In sentence B, the writer has not hesitated to insert "I," "you," and "your.")

29 Which of the following sentences are *personal*? _____

    A. This letter is to acknowledge receipt of the letter of July 8 and to inform those concerned that proper action has been taken.

    B. I'm sorry to tell you that we have decided to award the contract to Mr. Halloway.

    C. I'm happy to tell you that we have credited your account with $189.17.

    D. A decision to use the heat-sealing packaging process has been reached, and orders for the necessary equipment will be forthcoming.

B and C

These, we feel, are the eight qualities of an effective business letter. It must be easy to understand; that is, it must be *clear, concise, forceful*, and *well organized*. And it must have proper tone, by being *natural, friendly, courteous*, and *personal*.

The remaining chapters of this book are designed to help you inject these qualities into your letters by teaching you some of the knowledge and skills necessary for writing effective business letters.

A FINAL WORD ABOUT THIS BOOK

In this course, we won't suggest that there is only one way to say something. Nor will we teach you to write prefabricated sentences in formula letters. On the contrary, if you judiciously apply our principles and techniques, you will express your ideas in your *own way*—but more effectively.

Furthermore, you should not compare the principles and techniques found in this book with the rules of grammar. They are not similar. Most of the sentences you will be rewriting are not grammatically incorrect; rather, they contain faults which hinder the reader's understanding and make business writing ineffective. There may be several good solutions to a writing problem—some better than others. The principles and techniques in this book have been used by excellent writers for centuries. They require the writer to use a great deal of judgment and skill when he applies them in a specific situation.

Who casts to write a living line, must sweat.

It's true. There is no quick, easy road to effective letter writing. As any professional will tell you, writing is a very complex activity. Even experts try to improve.

Because good writing is so difficult, you must practice continually. In this course, we will be able to give you only a limited amount of practice in the exercise sections which follow each lesson. This means you will have to practice what you learn here in your own everyday correspondence.

HELPFUL HINT

The first step in learning to write effectively is to recognize faults in your own writing. Therefore, why don't you take a hard look at some of your recent business letters and ask yourself if they contain the eight qualities of an effective business letter? Ask yourself . . .

Is it clear?
Is it concise?
Is it forceful?
Is it well organized?
Is it natural?
Is it friendly?
Is it courteous?
Is it personal?

"Oh sure, I have your letter right in front of me."
By Severino Marcelo, Creative Book Services, New York.

PART ONE
WRITING THAT IS EASY
TO UNDERSTAND

The ten chapters of Part 1 will concentrate on helping
you make your writing easy to understand; that is, clear,
concise, and forceful.

ONE
TEST FOR CORRECTNESS
AND WORDINESS

There should be two main objects in ordinary prose
writing: to convey a message, and to include in it
nothing that will distract the reader's attention or check
his habitual pace of reading—he should feel that he is
seated at ease in a taxi, not riding a temperamental horse
through traffic.

Robert Graves and Alan Hodge

Use your mask here. Be sure to uncover the frame as far as the answer line.

1   Examine these letters:

A.   Dear Mr. Mickleton:

After carefully and painstakingly studying six sets of proposals, the members of our committee have selected your extremely unique lesson plans for our in-house course on the basic fundamentals of accounting. I wish to offer my congratulations!

I suggest that you look over the enclosed contract. In the event that you find that it meets with your approval, sign it and return it to me at this office.

In view of the fact that many details of design remain to be worked out, I hope we can meet sometime during the coming week. I'll give you a call early in the morning of Tuesday to arrange a conference.

Sincerely yours,

B.   Dear Mr. Mickleton:

After carefully studying six sets of proposals, our committee has selected your unique lesson plans for our in-house course on basic accounting. Congratulations.

Look over the enclosed contract. If you find it satisfactory, sign and return to me.

Since many details remain to be worked out, I hope we can meet sometime next week. I'll give you a call early on Tuesday to arrange a conference.

Sincerely yours,

Which letter is more effective? _____

B (Letter B has all eight qualities of an effective letter. Most important, it is much more concise than letter A—every word counts. Although letter A has good organization and a certain awkward friendliness, it is filled with words and phrases that make it windy and stilted.)

CORRECTNESS

2   From force of habit, we often use words or phrases that become obstacles to the reader's understanding and goodwill. In this chapter, we'll discuss how to detect some of these troublemakers and how to eliminate them. One way you can learn to test your words and phrases is to examine your *own* letters and ask yourself these questions:

Is it correct?
Is it necessary?
Is it wordy?

Let's begin with some examples that apply to the first question. Correct writing, like good manners, is not noticeable, but incorrect writing will distract your reader's attention from what you say and undermine his confidence in your capabilities. For example, look at the following sentence:

We will buy the computer *irregardless* of the cost.

"Irregardless" is not listed in your dictionary. "Regardless" is correct. Fill in the correct word in the next sentence:

We hope to go ahead with our plans irrespective of present difficulties and _____ of future obstacles.

---

regardless (We all tend to use "irregardless" occasionally, because "irrespective" *is* a correct word.)

3 "Irregardless" and similar incorrect usages distract your reader. Using a dictionary when necessary, begin to test your *own* words and phrases. Are they always correct?

"Unique" is another word often used incorrectly. "Unique" cannot be qualified. It means one of a kind, without equal. There are no *degrees* of "uniqueness."

Incorrect: This is a *most* unique problem.
Correct: This is a *unique* problem.

Rewrite the following sentence:

He has a most completely unique ability.

He has a *unique* ability.

Throughout this course you will be rewriting sentences and checking your answer with ours. Remember, your revision does not have to be worded *exactly* like our answer to be correct. As long as you have eliminated the fault under discussion, consider your answer correct. For instance, if you had rewritten the above sentence as, "His ability is unique," you would be correct. But if you wrote, "He has a *very* unique ability," then your answer would be wrong.

4a "Affect" and "effect" are often confused. "Affect" means "to influence." "Effect" means "to bring about." Choose one:

High costs adversely (affected/effected) prices. _____

---

affected

4b Poor salesmanship will (affect/effect) sales. _____

---

affect

5 "Affect" means "_____."

---

to influence

6   "Effect," as a noun, means "result"; as a verb, it means "to bring about."
"Affect" *cannot* be used as a noun.

   A.   They are satisfied with the (affects/effects) of the lighting. _____
   B.   You should (affect/effect) the changes immediately. _____

   A.   effects
   B.   effect

7   "_____" means "to influence."
   As a noun, "_____" means "_____." As a verb it
   means "_____."

   affect
   effect
   result
   to bring about

8   A.   His speech had a stimulating (affect/effect) on the audience. _____
   B.   When you hire this man, he will (affect/effect) the whole structure of the
        organization. _____
   C.   United Gas Corporation's research (affected/effected) a complete revolu-
        tion in oil refining practices. _____

   A.   effect (result)
   B.   affect (influence)
   C.   effected (brought about)

9   "Literally" is often incorrectly used to support a metaphor.

   Incorrect: The instructor's magnetism *literally* drew the new salesmen into a
               surrounding group.

"Literally" means "in fact." It is incorrect in the above sentence because a metaphor is a *non*-fact—the instructor's magnetism did not really "draw" the salesmen.
Rather, they literally walked over to him. Rewrite the sentence. _____

You are correct if you omitted "literally."

   The instructor's magnetism drew the new salesmen into a surrounding group.

10   The little word "fact" is often used incorrectly. Only statements which are
subject to direct verification are *facts.*

   A.   George Washington was the best President of the United States.
   B.   George Washington was the first President of the United States.
   C.   George Washington was the most intelligent President of the United
        States.

Which of these statements can be called a fact? _____

   B (Can you *directly verify* Washington's comparative intelligence or ability?
   Even though many people believe he was the best and most intelligent Presi

dent and even though you can amass much evidence to support these asser-
tions, you would not call the other two statements facts.)

11a Can this statement about the employment policies be called a fact?_____

Mr. Dewers summarized his report by stating the following fact: the new
employment policies will increase production by at least 10 percent.

No

11b What word should be correctly substituted for "fact" in the above sentence?

_____

**If you answered with any one of the following words, you are correct.
You may also consider yourself correct if your answer is a reasonable
synonym. This will be true of future questions as well.**

opinion, prediction, idea, thought

12 "Etc." means "and so on." Don't use "and etc." It's redundant.

The customer bought flash bulbs, reflectors, film, developer, (and etc./etc.)

_____

etc.

13 "Its" (without the apostrophe) is the possessive pronoun, as in, *its location,
its meaning.* "It's" (with the apostrophe) is the contraction of "it is" or "it has," as
in, *It's a nice day* or *It's been a nice day.* There is no such form as "its' "—with the
apostrophe *after* the "s."

A. (Its/It's/Its') going to be a big problem. _____

B. They found two of (its/it's/its') wheels in the rear of the factory. _____

A. It's

B. its

UNNECESSARY WORDS AND PHRASES

14a Correct writing is not necessarily effective writing, but effective writing is
always correct. Any time you are in doubt about one of your own words or
phrases, ask yourself this question:

Is it correct?

Then refer to a dictionary or a book on grammar.

However, some of your words and phrases may be "correct," but they may be
unnecessary to the meaning of your sentence.

The report was delayed because of the fact that the writer lost his rough draft
two days before the deadline.

Has "fact" been used correctly in this sentence? _____

Yes (The writer's loss can be directly verified.)

14b   But there is a criticism which can be leveled against "the fact that." Is it necessary to the meaning of the sentence? _____

   No

14c   Rewrite the sentence so that it is concise. _____

   The report was delayed because the writer lost his rough draft two days before the deadline.

15   Unnecessary words and phrases hamper your reader. He wants to know *as quickly as possible* what you are saying.

   Mr. Wright is studying along the line of aerodynamics.

What phrase can you eliminate from the above sentence without changing its meaning? _____

   along the line of

16   What are the unnecessary words below? _____

   Your first premium payment will be due on or before June 16.

   on or before

17   What words are *not* necessary below? _____

   I wish to tell you that the policy changes are excellent.

   I wish to tell you that

WORDINESS

18   Let's consider a third question: Is it *wordy*? Often, you can use fewer words to convey the meaning of a necessary but *wordy* phrase.

   May we hear from you *at an early date*?

This phrase is "necessary" because the meaning of the sentence would be changed if it was eliminated. Nevertheless, the sentence is not concise, because the phrase is wordy.

   May we hear from you _____?

   soon, shortly

19   Shorten this sentence. _____

   He takes inventory in order to keep occupied.

Is the *meaning* of your rewrite exactly the same as the meaning of our correct answer? If it isn't, your answer is incorrect.

   He takes inventory to keep occupied (to keep busy).

20 What is the word that should be substituted for the wordy phrase in this sentence?_____

Mr. Culver wrote me in connection with your job application.

about, regarding, concerning (Replaces "in connection with.")

21 Here are two examples of trite and wordy usage:

A. The facts, *as stated below*, speak for themselves.

B. The facts, *as stated above*, speak for themselves.

In A, just say "The following facts speak for themselves."

In B, just say _____ .

Any sentence which shows the reader where the facts are located and which does not have "as stated above" is correct.

These facts speak for themselves.

or

The above (preceding) facts speak for themselves.

22 What single word will replace the wordy phrase in the following sentence?____

In the normal course of procedure, we send out 250,000 invitations in May.

normally, usually, ordinarily, routinely (Replaces "In the normal course of procedure.")

23 A concise substitute for "at the present time" would be _____.

now, right now, presently

24a Is this phrase correct? _____

Mrs. Marvin hopes we *answer in the affirmative.*

Yes

24b Is it necessary?_____

Yes

24c Is it wordy? _____

Yes

24d Reduce "answer in the affirmative" to two words._____

say (answer) yes, answer affirmatively

25 Rewrite this sentence by reducing the *two* wordy phrases. _____

Because the box is too large in size, you will have to pack the apples over again.

Because the box is too *large*, you will have to pack the apples *again* (over).

or

Because the box is too *large*, you will have to *repack* the apples.

DOUBLETS

26   Some phrases are wordy simply because they say the same thing twice; they are *redundant*.

   Doublet: We must get to the *basic fundamentals* of the problem.

By definition, fundamentals are basic. There is no need to repeat yourself.

   Mr. Patterson has done well since he first began working for us.

What word in the above sentence should you cross out?_____

---

   first

27   I personally feel that Mr. Johnson is the best man for the job.

   In the above, "personally feel" is a doublet, because feelings or opinions can't be anything but personal. Thus, "personally" is not necessary. What word is not necessary in the following? _____

   I personally think that the new designs are too complicated.

---

   personally

28   Phrases such as "basic fundamentals" or "first began" are called *doublets*. There are two doublets in the next sentence. Rewrite it to eliminate the redundancy. _____

   The polite and courteous research team gave us their opinion based on the true facts.

   The *polite* (or *courteous*, but not both) research team gave us their opinion based on the *facts*.

29   Rewrite the following to get rid of the doublet. _____

   Avoid redundant doublets.

   Avoid doublets (redundancy).

   The incorrect, unnecessary, and wordy usages you just studied are samples of those that can occur in everyone's writing. If you wish to improve the quality of your letters, you must first develop the ability to recognize these kinds of defects. Only then will you acquire skill in eliminating them through revision.

   Such revision is always a difficult task, particularly for business people with limited time and a heavy work load. But a critical look at your first draft will eventually pay dividends in good writing habits. After you acquire these essential habits and skills, you will soon discover that many defects begin to disappear, even from the first draft.

Now begin the exercises.

EXERCISES

A   The following exercises will give you some practice in correct writing. Not all the specific points in this exercise were covered in the programmed part of the chapter, so don't hesitate to consult a reference book if you need to.

Use your mask here.

1   Each provision will be (affected/effected) by existing tax laws in your state.

affected

2   This (type/type of) contract is best for you. In fact, (its/it's/its') essential for your survival.

type of
it's

3   These men have (extremely unique/unique) abilities.

unique

4   There will be a meeting next Thursday (regardless/irregardless) of how many members will be there. Be sure to remind them to bring paper, pencils, I.D. cards, (etc./and etc.)

regardless
etc.

5   Many of our clients are extremely honest and well intentioned. We must always keep this (idea/fact) in mind.

idea

6   We were (literally/completely) petrified with fear.

completely

7   The school (principal/principle) stood by his (principals/principles).

principal
principles

8   I am (all ready/already) to type.

all ready

9   It is (all right/alright) to distribute the report.

all right

10   The supervisor was finally able to gather his workmen (all together/altogether) for a pep talk.

all together

B   Make the following sentences clear, concise, and forceful by eliminating unnecessary words and phrases and by shortening wordy phrases. Remember, not all the faulty words and phrases in these sentences were covered in the chapter. Take your time to make sure you don't miss any.

Use your mask here.

1 Due to the fact that the order for thirty cases of Musky Perfume will arrive during the coming week, you must repeat the collection routine over again and relay the order to our office at the earliest possible date.

Your sentence need not be exactly the same as ours, but in rewriting this sentence you should have . . .

1 Shortened "due to the fact that"
2 Shortened "during the coming week"
3 Eliminated "over again"
4 Shortened "at the earliest possible date"

> *Because* the order for thirty cases of Musky Perfume will arrive *next week*, you must repeat the collection routine and relay the order to our office *as soon as possible.*

2 In view of Mr. Lepofsky's opinion with regard to the Phelps case, we have asked Mr. Phelps to cooperate to the extent that he provide a birth certificate.

Remember, your revision does not have to compare word for word with ours for you to be correct, but in rewriting this sentence, you should have . . .

1 Shortened "in view of"
2 Shortened "with regard to"
3 Shortened "to the extent that"

> *Because* of Mr. Lepofsky's opinion *of* the Phelps case, we have asked Mr. Phelps to cooperate *by* providing a birth certificate.

3 In connection with your request to print the tally sheet, I called Johnson Printers on the occasion of my arrival in New York and ordered 1,500 copies to be delivered on or before June 17.

You should have . . .

1 Shortened "in connection with"
2 Shortened "on the occasion of"
3 Shortened "on or before"

> *About* your request to print the tally sheet, I called Johnson Printers *when* I arrived in New York and ordered 1,500 copies to be delivered *by* June 17.

4 During the time that you were visiting the Richmond property, management decided to abandon the policies followed in the normal course of procedure and introduced a new set of rules, which apply to all personnel at the present time.

You should have . . .

1 Shortened "during the time that"
2 Shortened "in the normal course of procedure"
3 Shortened or omitted "at the present time"

> *While* you were visiting (during your visit to) the Richmond property, management decided to abandon the policies *usually* followed and introduced a new set of rules, which (now) apply to all personnel.

5 For the above stated reasons, I wish to tell you that our department has started an investigation along the line of a possible reduction of overhead.

You should have . . .

1 Shortened "above stated"
2 Eliminated "I wish to tell you that"
3 Shortened "along the line of"

> For the *above* (these) reasons, our department has started an investigation *of* a possible reduction in overhead.

C Here is the ineffective letter you read at the beginning of this chapter:

> Dear Mr. Mickleton:
>
>   1   2
> After *carefully and painstakingly* studying six sets of proposals, the *members*
>
>   3
> *of our committee* have selected your *extremely unique* lesson plans for our
>
>   4   5
> in-house course on the *basic fundamentals* of accounting. *I wish to offer you*
>
> *my* congratulations!
>
>   6   7
> *I suggest that you* look over the enclosed contract. *In the event* that you find
>
>   8   9
> *that it meets with your approval*, sign it and return it to me *at this office*.
>
>   10   11
> *In view of the fact that* many details of design remain to be worked out, I
>
>   12
> hope we can meet sometime *during the coming week*. I'll give you a call early
>
>   13
> *in the morning* on Tuesday to arrange a conference.

The ineffective words and phrases in the previous letter have been numbered. Label each with the word "incorrect," "unnecessary," or "wordy."

1 _____	6 _____	11 _____
2 _____	7 _____	12 _____
3 _____	8 _____	13 _____
4 _____	9 _____	
5 _____	10 _____	

1 wordy (a doublet)	6 unnecessary	11 unnecessary
2 wordy	7 wordy	12 wordy
3 incorrect	8 wordy	13 unnecessary
4 wordy (a doublet)	9 unnecessary	
5 unnecessary	10 wordy	

D Rewrite the following sentences without doublets:

1 Our each and every wish is to assist our customers with thought and consideration.

Our *only* (*every, one*) wish is to assist our customers with *consideration.*

2 I personally feel that a report is not right and proper unless there is a full and complete statement of objectives.

I *feel* that a report is not *right* (*proper*) unless there is a *full* (*complete*) statement of objectives.

3 When they first began to promote dental hygiene, they came upon the same identical problem.

When they *began* to promote dental hygiene, they came upon the *same* problem.

4 Proxmire endorsed the back of the check, even though the pajamas were too large in size.

Proxmire *endorsed* the check, even though the pajamas were too *large.*

5 I returned back to my first point for extra special emphasis.

I *returned* to my first point for *special* emphasis.

HELPFUL HINT

After you finish writing your next letter, go over it carefully and ask yourself these three questions.

Is it correct?
Is it necessary?
Is it wordy?

If you find some word or phrase you aren't sure of, look it up in a reference book.

TWO

TEST FOR ARCHAIC, INFLATED, OR TOO TECHNICAL WORDS AND PHRASES

As a professional writer, I knew writing to be an art—first, last, and always. But also, as a writer who had started out to be a chemist, I did not despise a scientific approach. Early readability research made it clear that successful writing is somewhat systematic. There are limits relating to long sentences and long words that the craftsman does not go beyond.

Robert Gunning, Robert Gunning Associates

Use your mask here. Be sure to uncover the frame as far as the answer line.

1 Read these two letters:

A. Dear Mr. Stenger:

Enclosed you will herewith find two copies of the legal deed attendant to your purchase of the Pennymaker property. Prior to signing the aforementioned copies, I deem it advisable that you read Clause 19 pertaining to right of easement with reference to your neighbor Mr. Pownal.

If this accords with acceptable conditions, affix your signature to both documents and forward the carbon copy to me not later than January 14.

B. Dear Mr. Stenger:

I am enclosing two copies of the deed for the Pennymaker property. Before you sign them, be sure to read Clause 19, which covers the right of easement for your neighbor, Mr. Pownal. Right of easement refers to Mr. Pownal's legal right to water his livestock at the East Pond on this property.

If you find this acceptable, please sign both copies and send the carbon to me before January 14.

Which letter is effective? _____

B (Letter B is clear and natural, while letter A is not. Letter A probably doesn't inform, because one can't be sure that the reader knows what "right of easement" is. Nor does it make a good impression, because the wordy and unnecessary phrases can't be easily understood. Look again at the pompous, inflated language such as "herewith," "attendant to," "prior to," "aforementioned," "deem it advisable," "accords with," and "affix.")

ARCHAIC WORDS AND PHRASES

2 In Chapter 1, we hope you learned to test your words and phrases by asking . . .

Is it correct?
Is it necessary?
Is it wordy?

In this chapter, you will learn to test your words and phrases by asking . . .

Is it archaic?
Is it inflated?
Is it too technical?

One common enemy of clear, natural writing is the *archaic* word or phrase. Archaic words and phrases were welcome fifty years ago but not today, for modern companies don't wish to appear old-fashioned. Perhaps you do not use the rusty "I beg to," but how about those in the left-hand column below?

Archaic Words	Modern Words
1 *As per* your letter of April 13 . . .	A. Read
2 Your letter has been *duly noted*.	B. According to
3 *You will herewith find* the material you asked for.	C. Here is

Match the archaic word or phrase with its modern counterpart.

1 _____

2 _____

3 _____

1 B
2 A
3 C

3 Revise the following phrase to eliminate the archaic expression. _____
In re the recently proposed merger, I think . . .

About (Concerning, Regarding) the recently proposed merger, I think . . .

4 Replace only the archaic part with modern words. _____
Pursuant to our agreement, I enclose our check for $1,000.

As we agreed, As agreed, According to our agreement

5 Revise this. _____
As per Rule 178, you must file Form 1088 before July 10.

According to Rule 178, you must file Form 1088 before July 10.
or
Rule 178 stipulates that you must file Form 1088 before July 10.

6 Your job résumé has been duly noted by me.
Instead of the dry "duly noted," why not thank the reader? Revise the above.

_____

Thank you for sending me your job résumé.
or
Thank you for letting me read your job résumé.

7 You will herewith find our brochure, entitled, "Job Opportunities in Computer Programming."
Revise the above to eliminate the archaic phrase. _____

Here is (Enclosed is) our brochure, entitled, "Job Opportunities in Computer Programming."

INFLATED WORDS AND PHRASES

> I notice that you use plain, simple language, short words, and brief sentences. That is the way to write English. It is the modern way and the best way. Stick to it.

Mark Twain, from a letter to a young friend

8   Unfortunately, many business writers do not follow Mr. Twain's advice. Instead, they try to impress their readers with *inflated* language, which calls attention to the writer's vocabulary instead of meeting the reader's needs. Examine the following:

We will hire you *subsequent to* the arrival of your application.

What is the simple, modest word which could replace "subsequent to"? _____

---

after, upon

9   The iron ore will arrive by rail *prior to* the deadline date.

What little word should replace this pompous, inflated phrase? _____

---

before

10   I deem it advisable that you hire Smedley immediately.

Think of a good substitute for the inflated phrase in this sentence and rewrite it.

_____

I suggest that you hire Smedley immediately.
or

I think you should hire Smedley immediately.

11   I am writing *with reference to* your application.

What is a good substitute in this case? _____

---

about, regarding, concerning

12a   Business writers often inflate a simple idea with the word "advise."

Mr. Hill has advised me that your cotton shipment will arrive by rail.

"Your cotton shipment will arrive by rail" is (advice/information). _____

---

information

12b   "To advise" is a perfectly good verb, but in the above case it inflates the sentence. So, use "advise" when you are giving advice, not information. Revise the above sentence. _____

Mr. Hill has *informed* (*written, told*, etc.) me that your cotton shipment will arrive by rail.

13   We are in receipt of your check.

Why make this sentence so stiff? Make it simple and natural. _____

We *received* your check.

14a I regret to inform you that . . .

Is this inflated language? _____

Yes

14b Deflate it. _____

I am sorry that . . .

TECHNICAL WORDS

15 The *technical* word or phrase often impedes understanding. Technical words are simply those words which have a special meaning to an expert but are not understood by most people. Some business writers, particularly professional people, unconsciously use their own technical terms in their letters because they don't consider a reader's background.

You can, of course, buy your stock on *margin.*

When someone buys stock on margin, he borrows part of the cost from his stockbroker. If the reader did not know this, he would be confused by the above sentence. Rewrite the sentence, eliminating the technical term. _____

You can, of course, borrow part of the cost of your stock from us (me, your broker).

16 Sometimes, it *is* necessary to use a technical word for legal or other reasons. But always keep your reader in mind. If you think he may not know its meaning, provide him with an explanation or definition.

Mr. Douglas, your insurance policy has a grace period of thirty-one days. This means that you have a period of thirty-one days during which an overdue premium payment may be paid without penalty, while the policy remains in force.

Some writers defend their use of inflated language by calling it "technical." But often, it isn't technical; it's just inflated, as in the following:

As requested by your memorandum, this office has initiated an analyzation of our work schedule for the six months just past.

The words in the "Inflated" column below can be replaced by the words in the "Simple" column. Match them.

Inflated	*Simple*
1 As requested by your memorandum	A. to analyze
2 this office has initiated	B. the last six months
3 an analyzation	C. we have begun
4 the six months just past	D. as you asked

1 _____

2 _____

3 _____

4 _____

1 D
2 C
3 A
4 B

(The sentence now reads: "As you asked, we have begun to analyze our work schedule of the last six months.")

Now begin the exercises.

EXERCISES

A Each word or phrase in the column on the right is a modern substitute for a word or phrase in the column on the left. Match them.

Inflated or Archaic	*Modern and Concise*
1 Kindly	A. Instead of
2 Advise us	B. Soon
3 Tender	C. Say
4 This will acknowledge your	D. Please
5 Endeavor	E. Thank you for
6 In view of the fact that	F. Now
7 Under date of	G. If
8 In lieu of	H. As you asked
9 In the amount of	I. Since, because
10 We deem it advisable	J. For
11 State	K. Let us know
12 Not in a position to	L. We suggest
13 In compliance with your request	M. We think
14 It is our opinion	N. Delay
15 At the present time	O. Offer, send
16 Under separate cover	P. Try
17 In the event that	Q. Like
18 In the near future	R. Separately
19 Similar to	S. On
20 Inadvertent postponement	T. Cannot

Use your mask here.

1	D	11	C
2	K	12	T
3	O	13	H
4	E	14	M or L
5	P	15	F
6	I	16	R
7	S	17	G
8	A	18	B
9	J	19	Q
10	L or M	20	N

B The following ten sentences are filled with words and phrases which are incorrect, unnecessary, wordy, archaic, or inflated. Rewrite them so that they are clear, concise, and forceful. Remember that in each case our answer is only an example of several effective versions. There are only ten sentences to rewrite, so take your time. If you get off to a false start on a revision, cross it out and start over.

1 Because of the fact that we personally visited forty of the new radar installations, we were able to find eight major causes of equipment breakdown as stated below.

Consider your revision completely correct if you . . .

1 Omitted "of the fact that"
2 Omitted "personally"
3 Shortened "as stated below"

> Because we visited forty of the radar installations, we were able to find the *following* eight major causes of equipment breakdown.

2 In accordance with your request, attached please find our financial statement giving sales volume prior to February 12.

Your answer is completely correct if you . . .

1 Simplified and shortened "In accordance with your request"
2 Simplified "attached please find"
3 Substituted "before" for "prior to"

> *As you asked, I am enclosing* our financial statement which gives the sales volume *before* February 12.

3 We have revised the contract pursuant to your recommendations, but I deem it advisable to have your lawyer examine paragraph four with regard to technical mistakes.

Make sure that the meaning of your rewrite is exactly the same as the meaning of the original. Your answer is completely correct if it is and if you . . .

1 Shortened and simplified "pursuant to your recommendations"
2 Deflated "I deem it advisable"
3 Substituted "for" for "with regard to"

> We have revised the contract *as* you recommended, but *I think you should* have your lawyer examine paragraph four *for* technical mistakes.

4 We are in receipt of a letter from Mr. Paine, who says that his manuscript is still subject to revision.

Since the original sentence is not quite clear, your revision does not have to have exactly the same meaning. However, you are not completely correct unless you . . .

1 Simplified "in receipt of"
2 Simplified "is . . . subject to"

> *We received* a letter from Mr. Paine, who says that his manuscript *must be revised.*
>
> or
>
> Mr. Paine wrote that he is still revising his manuscript.

5 We have initiated an expense account program which will reduce our financial burden, taxwise, and which will also be in accordance with our needs on the matter of reduced entertainment expenses.

You are correct if you . . .

1 Deflated "initiated"
2 Shortened and simplified "our financial burden, taxwise"
3 Omitted "in accordance with our needs on the matter of"

> We have *begun* an expense account program which will reduce both our *taxes* and entertainment expenses.

6 In re your order for thirty dozen double-strength martini mixers, we find ourselves with an extremely unique shipping problem.

Your answer is correct if you . . .

1 Eliminated "In re"
2 Corrected "extremely unique"

> We find ourselves with a *unique* problem in shipping your order for thirty dozen double-strength martini mixers.
>
> or

About (*Concerning, Regarding*) your order for thirty dozen double-strength martini mixers, we find ourselves with a unique shipping problem.

7 You will herewith find the report of our chemist, who undertook the analyzation of several minerals with a nature resembling aluminum.

You are correct if you . . .

1 Simplified "you will herewith find"
2 Deflated "undertood the analyzation of"
3 Omitted "with a nature"

> *Enclosed is* (*Here is*) the report of our chemist, who *analyzed* several minerals resembling aluminum.

8 May we have at an early date your estimate along the line of copper tonnage needed for the purpose of constructing a new wiring system?

Check your revision to see if it says the same thing as the original. And you should have . . .

1 Shortened "at an early date"
2 Omitted "along the line of"
3 Shortened "for the purpose of"

> May we *soon* have your estimate of the copper tonnage needed *to* construct a new wiring system?

9 The Morton Company took your recommendations under advisement and are awaiting your favor with reference to a contract.

You are correct if you . . .

1 Deflated and shortened "took your recommendations under advisement"
2 Substituted "letter" for "favor"
3 Deflated "with reference to"

> The Morton Company *studied your recommendations* and are awaiting for your *letter about* a contract.

10 Will you be kind enough to effect the completion of this form and remit it to us on or before May 10?

You are correct if you . . .

1 Shortened "will you be kind enough to"
2 Simplified "effect the completion of"
3 Deflated "remit"
4 Simplified "on or before"

> *Please complete* this form and *send* it to us *by* May 10.

HELPFUL HINT

After you have written the first draft of your next letter, go over it word by word and phrase by phrase. Ask yourself these six questions:

Is it correct?
Is it necessary?
Is it wordy?
Is it archaic?
Is it inflated?
Is it technical?

At some point you may need a reference book. The following are very helpful.

> *A Dictionary of Modern English Usage*
> By H. W. Fowler
> Published by Oxford University Press
>
> *Writer's Guide and Index to English*
> By Porter G. Perrin
> Published by Scott, Foresman and Company

"I am afraid this is not a propitious time for a raise, Adams. Or, as my father would have said, why the devil should I give you a raise? Or, as my grandfather would have said, GET THE HECK OUT OF HERE!"

Drawing by Ed Arno, © 1971, Saturday Review, Inc.

WE DON'T DO IT THIS WAY ANY MORE

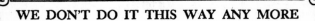

Reply—Congratulating a Firm Who Have
Overcome Their Difficulties

New York, Dec. 5th, 18___.

Gentlemen—We beg to acknowledge receipt of your esteemed favor of the 3d inst. The contents have given us great pleasure. We rejoice over the evidence of the prosperity of your house at last, after the dark shadow that so long hovered above it. It is refreshing to learn that you have succeeded in maintaining your position in the mercantile community, and are now sailing along again with the stream. Your success is a perpetual reminder to others that "Where there's a will there's a way." The energy and business tact which has superseded the old order of things must tell to the advantage of your house in the future; and you may rely upon us, as heretofore, to give our special attention to your demands when pleased to forward them. Until then, with many wishes for your success, we remain,

Yours truly,

Wright, Banks & Co.

—*Payne's Business Letter Writer and Book of Commercial Forms*, 1884

THREE
USE SPECIFIC ACTION VERBS

When Demosthenes was asked what was the first part of oratory, he answered, "action," and which was the second, he replied, "action," and which was the third, he still answered, "action."

Use your mask here.

1   Which of the two letters below is more effective?

A.   Dear. Mr. Farber:

As is probably your understanding, completion of Moviepix's production of "White Stallion" has been achieved by the crew, and the producer's plan is to have simultaneous premieres of the picture in the thirty big cities on September 17. However, a big New York theater is not yet under contract to show it.

Since "White Stallion" is a picture with special appeal to kids, it is the hope of the producer that Radio City Music Hall will be the picture's showplace. But if their schedule is already complete, RKO Palace and the Winter Garden are good alternatives in that order.

A preview copy should be in your office next week, ready for a showing to theater managers. It's a great picture and will do its own selling. And it is my understanding that you are well able to obtain Music Hall's acceptance.

Sincerely yours,

B.   Dear Mr. Farber:

As you probably know, the crew has completed Moviepix's production of "White Stallion," and the producer plans to hold simultaneous premieres in the thirty big cities on September 17. However, we have not yet signed a big New York theater to show it.

Since "White Stallion" should especially appeal to kids, the producer hopes you can land Radio City Music Hall. But if they're already booked, try RKO Palace and the Winter Garden in that order.

A preview copy should arrive in your office next week, so you can show it to theater managers. It's a great picture and will sell itself, but I know I can count on you to book it into the Music Hall.

Sincerely yours,

B (Letter B is more concise than A—twenty-five words shorter. In addition, it's more forceful—has more punch—primarily because it has specific action verbs. These vigorous verbs stand at the heart of each sentence, while feeble ones cripple those in letter A.)

Remember: always move your mask down to the answer line before you begin to read a frame.

IDENTIFYING ACTION AND BEING VERBS

2   To write forcefully, you must learn to distinguish between two kinds of verbs:

1 *Action verbs* express action.
2 *Being verbs** express a state of being.

Label each of the verbs in the following sentences according to type.

A. Mr. Quilty *fell*. _____
B. Bill *was struck* by the ball. _____
C. Mr. Hobart *is* at home. _____
D. He *will be* there. _____

A. action verb
B. action verb
C. being verb
D. being verb

3 Which sentence below has the action verb? _____

A. The committee *rejected* Miss Taylor's report.
B. Miss Woodward's report definitely *is* better.

A

4 Here is a list of sentences containing action verbs or being verbs. Which sentences contain the being verbs? _____

A. The nation was hit by a depression.
B. They are not in the office.
C. He was all right.
D. He fell sixty-eight floors.
E. Apparently he is ill.
F. They spoke to him regretfully.

B
C
E

5 What type of verb does this sentence have? _____

Negotiation of the terms of the agreement was Mr. Mileaf's purpose.

---

a being verb ("was")

6 What type of main verb does this sentence have? _____

When Mr. Mileaf was at the embassy, he wanted to negotiate the terms of the agreement.

---

an action verb ("wanted")

ACTION VERBS FOR BEING VERBS

7 Action interests your reader. To put action in your sentence, simply substitute an action verb for a being verb.

*Being verbs are also called *copula, copulative verbs, coupling verbs, joining verbs,* or *linking verbs.*

There was a week of discussion of commodity prices by the delegates.

The being verb "was" weakens the above sentence. Make it more lively by substituting an action verb in the sentence below.

The delegates _____ commodity prices for a week.

discussed

8a You can often make your sentences more forceful (and concise) by replacing a being verb with an action verb. Consider this sentence.

The high cost of raw materials has forced Sintex Corporation to raise its prices.

A being verb often indicates that a sentence is weak. Does this sentence have a being verb as the main verb? _____

No

8b Is it a forceful, effective sentence? _____

Yes (We think so.)

9a Now consider this sentence:

There was a demonstration of the new oscillator by Mr. Knight.

Is this a concise, forceful sentence? _____

No

9b What is the main verb of this sentence? _____

was

9c The above sentence is weak because it has a being verb. However, two elements of action hide in two of its nouns. One of these actions hides in the noun "oscillator." It can be converted to the verb, "to oscillate." See if you can find the other hidden action. It hides in a noun and you can convert it to the verb, "to _____."

demonstrate

9d Now, you want to replace the being verb, "was," with the action verb, "to demonstrate." Rewrite the above sentence by using "to demonstrate" as the main verb. _____

You are correct if your revision has the same meaning as the sentence above and if "to demonstrate" is the main verb.

Mr. Knight *demonstrated* the new oscillator.

or

The new oscillator *was demonstrated* by Mr. Knight.

10a Consider this sentence:

A quick reply to a customer's letter is necessary for a clerk.

What type of verb is the main verb of this sentence? _____

---

a being verb ("is")

10b The action in this sentence hides in a noun which can be converted to the action verb, "to _____ ."

---

reply

10c Now write a concise, forceful sentence by using "to reply" as the main verb.

You are correct if "to reply" or "to answer" is the main verb of your revision.

A clerk *must (should) reply* quickly to a customer's letter.

or

A customer's letter *must be answered* quickly by a clerk.

11a Now look at this sentence:

Faulty reproduction of the negatives is the cause of the decline in our picture quality.

This sentence is ineffective because the main verb is a being verb. However, *three* elements of action are camouflaged as nouns. The first noun of the sentence can be converted to the action verb, "to _____ ."

---

reproduce

11b Two other elements of action remain to be discovered. They are:

to _____

to _____

---

cause
decline

11c Now, to make the above sentence more forceful, we want to replace the being verb "is" with one of these action verbs. Let's try it with "to reproduce" first.

The negatives *were reproduced* with faults, causing the decline in picture quality.

Is this sentence more forceful and concise than the original?_____

Yes

11d Do the revision and the original sentence have the same meaning? _____

Yes

11e But let's see if we can do even better by using "to decline" for the main verb.

Picture quality *declined* because the negatives were reproduced with faults.

Is this revision more concise than the first revision?_____

Yes (It's two words shorter.)

11f   Do both revisions have the same meaning?_____

Yes

11g   There is still one more way to revise the original sentence. Using "to cause" for the main verb, write a third version. _____

You are correct if "to cause" is the main verb of your revision.

Faulty reproduction of the negatives *caused* the decline in picture quality.

or

The decline in picture quality *was caused* by faulty reproduction of the negatives.

or

Faulty reproduction of the negatives *caused* picture quality *to decline*. (Thus, you can see that using "to cause" as the main verb gives the most forceful and concise revision of all.)

12a   Take a look at these two sentences:

A.   Fifty sets of Gillen dinnerware were shipped to Farnam's department store in time for their July 10 opening.

B.   A feature of the Thinktight Computer is its capacity to bring about a solution of a mathematical problem in one one-thousandth of a second.

One of these sentences is not effective. By this time, you should know what the telltale sign is. So test each sentence. Which sentence lacks force?_____

B (Sentence B has a being verb.)

12b   Sentence B has several sources of hidden action. But see if you can pick the *best* action right away. It is "to _____ ."

Also consider yourself correct if you answered with "to feature" or "to bring (about)." But you will soon see that these two action verbs do not produce the *best* revision.

solve

12c   Let's experiment with all three action verbs. Using "to feature" as the main verb will not produce a very effective revision. The following is about the best anyone can do.

The Thinktight Computer *features* a capacity to bring about a solution of a mathematical problem in one one-thousandth of a second.

See if you can do better by using "to bring about" as the main verb of your revision. _____

Consider yourself correct if "to bring about" is the main verb.

The Thinktight Computer *can bring about* the solution of a mathematical problem in one one-thousandth of a second.

12d So far, this is the better revision, because it's six words shorter than the original sentence and more forceful. But see if you can do even better by using "to solve" as the main verb. _____

Consider yourself correct if "to solve" is the main verb of your sentence.

The Thinktight Computer *can solve (solves)* a mathematical problem in one one-thousandth of a second.

13a Here's another example:

Completion of the project by us is necessary for this month.

What indicates that this sentence may be weak? _____ (Your own words)

The main verb "is" is a being verb.

13b The hidden action in this sentence is "to _____."

complete

13c Now, before you rewrite the above sentence, consider what subject you are going to attach to the action verb. Two possibilities exist. One is the person or thing doing the action in the sentence and the other is the person or thing acted upon. What is the thing acted upon? _____

the project (the thing being completed)

13d Rewrite the above sentence using "project" as the subject and "to complete" as the main verb. _____

You are correct if "project" is the subject and "to complete" is the main verb of your revision.

The *project must (should) be completed* (by) this month (by us).

13e Who or what is doing the action in the above sentence?_____

us, we

13f Rewrite the above sentence using "we" as the subject and "to complete" as the main verb.

You are correct if "we" is subject and "to complete" is the main verb of your revision.

We must (should) complete the project this month.*

14a What is the hidden action in the following? _____

The color code is a factor in helping the engineer.

help

*In Chapter 4, we will discuss active vs. passive sentences.

14b   What are the two possible subjects of your revision? _____

(color) code (thing doing the action)
engineer (person acted upon)

14c   Write *two* effective versions of the above sentence. _____

You are correct if "to help" is the main verb of both your sentences and if "code" is the subject of one and "engineer" is the subject of the other.

The *color code* helps the engineer. ("Code" is the person or thing *doing* the action.)

or

The *engineer is helped* by the color code. ("Engineer" is the person or thing *acted upon*.)

SPECIFIC VERBS FOR GENERAL VERBS

15a   Some action verbs are more *specific* than others and, consequently, more forceful. Look at these verbs:

A. were
B. increased
C. climbed

Which is the most specific? _____

C

15b   Which of the following sentences is most forceful? _____

A. The market averages *were* up four points on Thursday.
B. The market averages *increased* by four points on Thursday.
C. The market averages *climbed* four points on Thursday.

C

16a   Look at these two verbs:

A. to go
B. to mail

Are these action verbs? _____

Yes

16b   Which action verb is more specific? _____

B (There are many ways to "go.")

16c   Now look at these two sentences:

A. The sales manager's message *went* to the West Coast office on Monday
B. The sales manager's message *was mailed* to the West Coast office on Monday.

Do both these sentences have action verbs? _____

Yes

16d Which sentence is not only more forceful but more informative? _____

B (Its action verb is more specific.)

17 Here is a list of action verbs. Some are more specific than others. Choose the specific action verbs. _____

A. to accomplish
B. to dash
C. to cling
D. to achieve
E. to repair
F. to effect

B
C
E

18a Consider this sentence:

The delivery of the stock certificates should be accomplished by you not later than noon, Thursday.

Is the main verb of this sentence an action verb? _____

Yes

18b Is the main verb of this sentence general or specific? _____

general

18c The *specific* action hides in the noun, " _____ ".

delivery

18d If "to deliver" is to be the main verb of your revision, what are the two subject possibilities? _____

stock certificates
you

18e Now write *two* forceful versions of the above sentence. _____

You are correct if both your revisions have "to deliver" as the main verb and if the subject of one is "stock certificates" and the subject of the other is "you."

You should deliver the stock certificates not later than (by) noon, Thursday.

or

The *stock certificates should be delivered* by you not later than noon, Thursday.

(Compare both these revisions with the original sentence.)

19a Placement was achieved by the janitor in the case of four bulletin boards which are in the recreation room.

The main verb of this sentence, "was achieved," is a _____ action verb.

---

general

19b What is the specific action hidden in the sentence?_____

---

place (placement)

19c Write *two* forceful versions of the above sentence. _____

You are correct if both your revisions have "to place" as the main verb and if the subject of one is "janitor" and the subject of the other is "bulletin boards."

The *janitor placed* four bulletin boards in the recreation room.

and

Four *bulletin boards were placed* by the janitor in the recreation room.

20a You can see, then, that the being verb is not the only indicator of weak sentences. So, when you test the main verb, you should check to see if it is a being verb *or* a general action verb. Both sentences below can be improved. Which has the general action verb?_____

A. Some reduction of costs was effected by this office early this month.
B. There are certain problems which confront the panel.

A ("was effected")

20b What type of verb is in sentence B?_____

---

being verb ("are")

20c In sentence A, the hidden specific action is "to _____ ."
In sentence B, the hidden action is "to _____ ."

---

reduce

confront

20d Write *two* forceful and concise versions of sentence A._____

You are correct if "to reduce" is the main verb of both your sentences and if "office" is the subject of one and "costs" is the subject of the other.

This *office (partly) reduced* costs early this month.

and

Some *costs were reduced* by this office early this month.

20e Write two forceful and concise versions of sentence B. _____

You are correct if "to confront" is the main verb of both your sentences and if "problems" is the subject of one and "panel" is the subject of the other.

> Certain *problems confront* the panel.
>
> and
>
> The *panel is confronted* by certain problems.

21 At the trade fair, the Scurry-Meadows model home was the favorite exhibit of the delegates.

This sentence is made ineffective by the being verb "was." See if you can fill in an appropriate action verb in the following revision.

> Of all the exhibits at the trade fair, the delegates _____ the Scurry-Meadows model home the best (most).

favored, liked, appreciated, admired

22 Study this first-draft sentence.

> The new restrictions will be under the committee's careful examination.

Write *two* concise and forceful versions of the above sentence. _____

If "to examine" is the main verb of both your sentences and if "committee" is the subject of one and "restrictions" is the subject of the other, you are correct.

> The *committee will* carefully *examine* the new restrictions.
>
> and
>
> The new *restrictions will be* carefully *examined* by the committee.

23a An agreement of the three negotiators occurred on May 16.

Is the main action verb of the above sentence general or specific? _____

general ("occurred")

23b What is the hidden action? _____

to agree

23c Write a concise, forceful version of the above sentence. _____

You are correct if "to agree" is your main verb.

> On May 16, the three *negotiators agreed* (on May 16).

24a Now consider this sentence.

> *Loss* of 50 percent of your capital *was* the result of an accident *which came about* in a collision of two trucks on the thruway.

This sentence has *two* subject-verbs. The subject-verb of the main statement is "loss ... was." The second subject-verb is found in the clause. It is "which came about." The verb in the first subject-verb is a _____ .

---

being verb

24b The verb in the second subject-verb is a _____ .

---

general action verb

24c Certainly you can improve this sentence with several kinds of revisions. So take a moment and find the hidden action. Now rewrite the sentence once or twice. When you're satisfied that *all* your subjects are attached to specific action verbs, check below. _____

Most likely, your revision is not exactly the same as either of those below. However, consider yourself correct if *all* your subjects have action verbs.

You lost 50 percent of your capital when (because) *two* of your trucks (accidentally) *collided* on the thruway.

or

A thruway *accident* between two of your trucks *caused* you to lose 50 percent of your capital. (This revision is not as good as the first.)

Now begin the exercises.

EXERCISES

A Rewrite the following ten sentences so that they are concise and forceful. Keep this principle in mind:

When possible, replace being verbs and general action verbs with specific action verbs.

If you get off on the wrong foot with your revision, cross it out and try again before you look at the correct answer.

Use your mask here.

1 Fleepox Powder is a substance which can be of damage to your skin.

You are correct if you used "to damage" as your main verb.

Fleepox *Powder can damage* your skin.

or

Your *skin can be damaged* by Fleepox Powder.

2 Rapid gas flow is a factor for us to consider when we design the pipe system.

Your sentence does not have to be exactly the same as ours, but in rewriting this sentence, you should have used "to consider" as the main verb.

We should consider rapid gas flow when we design the pipe system.

3   Early last month, mechanization of the production line was established by the Riley Instrument Company.

You are correct if you used "to mechanize" as your main verb.

Early last month, the Riley Instrument Company *mechanized* the production line.

or

Early last month, the production *line was mechanized* by the Riley Instrument Company.

4   The gyrocompass system has an automatic feature of aligning the platform with the proper heading.

You are correct if you used "to align" for the main verb.

The gyrocompass *system* automatically *aligns* the platform with the proper heading.

5   The rod will be of great interest to Dr. Fortnight.

You should have used "to interest" as the main verb.

The *rod* will greatly *interest* Dr. Fortnight.

or

Dr. Fortnight will be greatly *interested* in the rod.

6   This sales message should be something of vital concern to all our personnel.

If your answer doesn't say the same thing as the original, it is incorrect. But if it does and if you used "to concern" as the main verb, you are correct.

This sales *message should* vitally *concern* all our personnel.

or

All our *personnel should be* vitally *concerned* with this sales message.

7   A certification of this agreement is one of our needs.

Notice that the two revisions below do not have exactly the same meaning because the sentence above has two interpretations: (1) we need a certification to be signed by someone, not necessarily ourselves. (2) We need to certify the agreement ourselves. However, consider yourself correct if you used "to need" for your main verb

We need a certification of this agreement.

or

We need to certify this agreement.

8 This contract has a requirement that it be signed by you by June 8.

You are correct if you used "to require" or "to sign" as your main verb.

This *contract requires* your signature by June 8.

or

You are required to sign this contract by June 8.

or

You must (should) sign this contract by June 8.

9 This makes it necessary for us to refuse your request with regret.

You are correct if you used "to refuse" or "to regret" for your main verb.

Regretfully, *we must refuse* your request.

or

We regret that *we must refuse* your request.

10 It is my opinion that . . .

I think (feel, believe) that . . .

B This exercise takes about twenty or thirty minutes to finish. If you have been working more than an hour on this chapter, perhaps you should take a break or do it some other time.

Below is the ineffective letter you read at the beginning of this chapter. It is not concise or forceful because most of its sentences have faulty verbs. Rewrite it sentence by sentence.

Dear Mr. Farber:

1 As is probably your understanding, completion of Moviepix's production of "White Stallion" has been achieved by the crew, and the producer's plan is to have simultaneous premieres of the picture in the thirty big cities on September 17. 2 However, a big New York theater is not yet under contract to show it.

3 Since "White Stallion" is a picture with special appeal to kids, it is the hope of the producer that Radio City Music Hall will be the picture's showplace. 4 But if their schedule is already complete, RKO Palace and the Winter Garden are good alternatives in that order.

5 A preview copy should be in your office next week, ready for showing to theater managers. 6 It's a great picture and will do its own selling. 7 And it is my understanding that you are well able to obtain Music Hall's acceptance.

Sincerely yours,

Now take a good look at your revision. Have you done everything you possibly can to make it effective? If yes, compare your letter with the effective revision below.

Dear Mr. Farber:

1 As *you* probably *know*, the *crew has completed* Moviepix's production of "White Stallion," and the *producer plans* to hold simultaneous premieres in the thirty big cities on September 17.

You should have . . .

1 Substituted the action hiding in "understanding" for the first being verb, "is,"
2 Substituted the action hiding in "completion" for the weak action verb, "has been achieved,"
3 Substituted the action hiding in "plan" for the second being verb, "is."

2 However, *we haven't signed* any big New York theater to show it.

You should have substituted some sort of action verb for the being verb, "is."

3 Since *"White Stallion" should* especially *appeal* to kids, the *producer hopes* you can land Radio City Music Hall.

You should have . . .

1 Substituted the action hidden in "appeal" for the first being verb, "is,"
2 Substituted the action hidden in "hope" for the second being verb, "is,"
3 Replaced the third being verb, "will be," with an appropriate action verb.

4 But if *they're* already *booked, try* RKO Palace and the Winter Garden in that order.

You should have . . .

1 Substituted some sort of action verb for the first being verb, "is"—"But if *they have* already *completed* their schedule" is a good alternative,
2 Substituted any appropriate action verb for the being verb, "are."

5 A preview *copy should arrive* in your office next week, so *you can show* it to theater managers.

You should have replaced the being verb, "should be," with an appropriate action verb.

6 It's a great picture and *will sell* itself, . . .

You should have substituted the action hidden in "selling" for the weak action verb, "will do."

7 . . . but *I know I can count* on you to book it into the Music Hall.

You should have . . .

1 Substituted the action hiding in "understanding" for the first being verb, "is,"
2 Replaced the being verb, "are," with an appropriate action verb.

HELPFUL HINT

---

1 When possible, replace being verbs with action verbs.
2 When possible, replace general action verbs with specific ones.

These are two of the most important principles that you can learn. If you conscientiously apply them to your own letters, you will eliminate, in one sweep, a multitude of writing ills. Your sentences will be more concise because specific action verbs automatically eliminate wordy or unnecessary phrases. Your letters will be more forceful because you reduce the number of "it is" and "there are" sentences.

So, after you write the first draft of your next business letter, test each sentence to see if it harbors a being verb or a general action verb. If so, you may not be writing as forcefully and concisely as you can. Improve each faulty sentence by finding the hidden action and using it as the main verb.

FOUR
MAKE YOUR SENTENCES ACTIVE

Perhaps the scarcest commodity among businessmen is time. Thus, the young person who has learned to save time by presenting his ideas clearly, concisely, and persuasively has taken a major step toward success. By devoting serious attention to the details of effective communication, he will be able to contribute significantly to his organization and promote his own career as well.

A. W. Clausen, President, Bank of America

Use your mask here.

ACTIVE AND PASSIVE SENTENCES

In Chapter 3, we showed you how to make your sentences more concise and forceful by using specific action verbs. In this chapter, we will show you how to improve your sentences by making them *active*. To do this, you must concentrate on the *subject*, not the verb.

1a A. The staff wrote the report.
  B. The report was written by the staff.

What word is the subject of sentence A? _____

  staff

1b What word is the subject of sentence B? _____

  report

1c The staff is the *doer of the action* in _____

  A. sentence A
  B. sentence B
  C. both sentences

  C

1d The doer of the action is the *subject* of _____

  A. sentence A
  B. sentence B
 .C   both sentences

  A

1e When the subject of a sentence is the doer of the action, that sentence is called an *active sentence.** Which sentence is the active sentence? _____

  A

2 Which sentence below is the active sentence? _____

  A. Professor Dalis will supervise the research project.
  B. The research project will be supervised by Professor Dalis.

  A

3a The agreement was initialed.

What word is the subject of the above? _____

  agreement

3b Is the subject of this sentence the doer of the action? _____

  No (The agreement is not doing the initialing.)

---

*Active sentence is a term used to describe one type of *sentence. Active voice* is a term used to identify a type of *verb.*

3c   Is this an active sentence? _____

No

4   When the subject of a sentence is *acted upon*, that sentence is a *passive* sentence. In which sentence below is the subject being acted upon? _____

    A.   The meeting was brought to order.

    B.   The meeting came to order.

A (It is the passive sentence.)

5   Label the following sentences as active or passive.

    A.   Feeling ran high. _____

    B.   The treaty was ratified. _____ ___

---

active

passive

6a   In Chapter 3, you learned about being verbs and action verbs.

    The contract was signed.

Is the main verb of this sentence an action verb? _____ ___

Yes ("was signed")

6b   Is it a passive sentence? _____

Yes (The subject is acted upon.)

6c   Is the main verb of the following sentence an action verb? _____

    Mr. Wendell signed the contract.

Yes

6d   Is it an active sentence? _____

Yes (The subject is doing the action.)

6e   An action verb may be found in _____

    A.   an active sentence

    B.   a passive sentence

    C.   both active and passive sentences

C

LINKING SENTENCES

7   If the main verb of a sentence is a being verb, that sentence is called a *linking* sentence. Label the following three sentences with the terms *active*, *passive*, and *linking*.

    A.   The interest was paid on June 11. _____

    B.   The interest is due on June 11. _____

    C.   Mr. Harriman paid the interest on June 11. _____

    A. passive
    B. linking
    C. active

8 The being verb in a linking sentence links the subject with an idea, as in:

His fee *is* reasonable.
The night shift *is* the more efficient work force.

Thus, a being verb shows a relationship rather than expresses any kind of action.

If your sentence is to be clear, your reader must learn at the very least: (1) who or what is doing what, (2) who or what is having what done to it, or (3) who or what is linked to whom or what. No matter how complex they become, all English sentences must clearly express one of these three skeleton statements. That is, they must have an active, passive, or linking form.

Identify the form of each sentence below:

    A. Further notices will be sent to you at your new address. _____
    B. We are returning the extra thirty-two cents in stamps. _____
    C. It was nice to see you. _____
    D. The customer was sent upstairs to the credit department. _____

    A. passive
    B. active
    C. linking
    D. passive

USE ACTIVE SENTENCES

9a Now read these two newspaper accounts:

    A. Man Plunges into Hudson

        Mr. Crane Hart, 43, of Lindhurst, plunged over the side of the ferry Piermont into the Hudson River shortly after midnight today. A passenger who saw him shouted "Man overboard!" Someone shone a flashlight over the water. Crew members launched two life rafts.

    B. Incident Reported

        Mr. Crane Hart, 43, of Lindhurst, was reported to have fallen from the ferry Piermont into the Hudson River shortly after midnight today. Witnessing the incident, a passenger was said to have shouted that a man was overboard. A flashlight was shone over the water by someone. Two life rafts were launched by crew members.

How many active sentences are there in paragraph A? _____
How many in paragraph B? _____

---

    four
    none

9b Which account is more concise? _____

    A (It's thirteen words shorter.)

9c Which account is more forceful?_____

> A (Most people must force themselves to read writing such as that in paragraph B, because the verbs are not specific and the sentences are passive. Too much of this kind of writing puts a modern reader to sleep. However, paragraph A has the kind of writing which helps make business letters effective. It is lively and interesting because it has many active sentences and specific action verbs.)

10a Weak writing has a high proportion of passive or linking sentences, but concise, forceful writing has many active sentences. Examine the following:

    A. The contract was approved by the president.
    B. The president approved the contract.

Do these two sentences have exactly the same meaning? _____

> Yes

10b Which one is more concise—the passive or the active sentence?_____

> the active sentence (It is two words shorter. Also, in any sentence, the reader's interest tends to drop off right after the main statement has been completed. But of course it's desirable to maintain his interest to the end of the sentence, if possible. Notice the main statement in the passive sentence. The reader's interest will drop off after the word "approved," but in the active sentence interest is sustained all the way to the end.)

11a Here is a new principle which will help you make your writing clearer, more concise, and more forceful.

When possible, replace passive and linking sentences with active sentences.

Let's try applying this to the following:

The report was written by Mr. Moriarity in three weeks.

What kind of sentence is this? _____

> a passive sentence

11b Who or what is doing the action? _____

> Mr. Moriarity

11c To make this sentence active, you must make "Mr. Moriarity" the subject. Do so. _____

You are correct if "Mr. Moriarity" is the subject and "to write" is the verb.

Mr. Moriarity wrote the report in three weeks.

12a What kind of sentence is this?_____

An attempt was made by the witness to evade the question.

> a passive sentence

12b Not only is this sentence passive, but it has a general action verb for the main verb. There's no excuse for this, since plenty of action hides in the sentence. The best hidden action is "to _____."

---

attempt, try

12c   The doer of this action is _____ .

(the) witness

12d   Now convert the sentence into an effective active sentence. _____

The *witness attempted* (tried) to evade the question.

13a   What kind of sentence is this? _____

The vital importance of this idea is a matter perfectly apparent to my understanding.

---

a linking sentence (The main verb is "is.")

13b   What is the hidden action? _____

---

to understand

13c   For practice, use this action to write a *passive* sentence. _____

You are correct if "importance" is the subject and "to understand" is the main verb.

The vital *importance* of this idea *is understood* (perfectly) by me.

13d   This passive revision is more concise and forceful than the original linking sentence, but make it even more effective by turning it into an active sentence.

I understand (perfectly) the vital importance of this idea.

14   Sometimes both the subject-verb of the main statement and the subject-verb of the modifying clause must be made active.

After ownership of this estate was transferred by us to Mr. Mendes, these forms were completed by him and returned with the deed to us.

Make *all* the subject-verbs in this sentence active. _____

After *we transferred* ownership of this estate to Mr. Mendes, *he completed* these forms and *returned* them with the deed to us.

15   Which of these statements is more nearly true? _____

A.   Linking sentences and passive sentences are always ineffective and should be replaced by active sentences.

B.   Although linking and passive sentences are often wordy and usually less forceful than active sentences, they *are* useful and necessary in some letter-writing situations.

B

16   As we mentioned before, linking sentences and being verbs are useful when you want to emphasize a relationship between the subject and an idea that has no action.

> Management Training 104 *is* an advanced course.

Linking verbs are also necessary when presenting logical relationships.

> Mr. Armbruster *is* a man. All men *are* mortal. Therefore, Mr. Armbruster *is* mortal.

The passive sentence also has several uses. At the end of paragraphs, it gives rhythm and pace to your writing. A long succession of active sentences can become monotonous. More important for business writers, the passive sentence has two primary functions. First, it is used when the writer simply doesn't know the doer of the action or when the doer isn't important, as in:

> Your credit application *has been approved.*

Also, the passive sentence is used when the writer doesn't want to identify the doer of an action, as in:

> Detrimental information about the applicant *has been supplied.*

Which of the following statements is more nearly true?_____

A. Most business writers use far too many passive and linking sentences, and the reader suffers accordingly. Writers would do well to concentrate on making a large majority of their sentences active.

B. Since passive and linking sentences are useful and necessary, a writer should have about an equal number of active, passive, and linking sentences in his letters.

A (It's true, most business writers use far too many passive and linking sentences. We think that about eight out of ten of your sentences should be active, because this is the kind of writing that conveys your message most quickly and efficiently. Pick up any magazine or newspaper that you admire and count the number of active sentences that appear in any paragraph. Or analyze the writing of your favorite author. Several studies of this subject show that active sentences outnumber passive sentences by about nine to one.)

THE NATURAL WRITING PROCESS

We hope that you are convinced and that from here on you will make most of your sentences active.

However, to apply any of the principles and techniques that you learned in this and previous chapters, you must learn to follow the *natural writing process.* For if you don't, you may become a victim of an occupational hazard called writer's paralysis. This dread disease is chiefly found among writers who are becoming critical and self-conscious of their writing (as we hope you are). However, at this point, a negative effect often sets in. There you sit, a blank sheet in front of you, pen poised—and you can't write a word because you're paralyzed by the thought that anything you try will be wrong.

This won't happen to you if you follow the *natural writing process*. This process involves three steps:

1 *Thinking* carefully of what you want to say
2 *Writing* your sentences to express your thoughts as best you can
3 *Revising* your sentences to express your thoughts effectively

Every good writer does this. He gets it down somehow. And only then does he begin to test his words and phrases, replace being verbs and general action verbs with strong action verbs, and convert to active sentences. These are revision activities.

Now begin the exercises.

EXERCISES

Rewrite the following passive and linking sentences so that they are active. Some of these sentences have more than one subject-verb. So remember to change all of them. Also, if the sentence you are revising is a linking sentence, remember to find the hidden action.

Use your mask here.

1 The lawsuit was settled by Mr. Cares.

Mr. Cares settled the lawsuit.

2 When this form is received by us, the change will be made.

You are correct if you . . .

1 Made "form is received" active
2 Made "change will be made" active

When *we receive* this form, *we (I) will make* the change.

or

We will make the change when *we receive* this form.

3 As you asked in our telephone conversation today, your name has been changed on our records.

As you asked in our telephone conversation today, *we (I) have changed* your name on our records.

4 The information has just been received by us.

The *information has just arrived.*

or

We (I) just received the information.

5 It is indicated that a diversification of products will be begun by this competitor.

You are correct if you . . .
1   Changed "it is indicated" to some sort of active form or to an adverb
2   Made "products will be begun" active

> Apparently, this *competitor will begin (start)* to diversify his products.
>
> or
>
> *It seems* (We think) that this *competitor will begin* to diversify his products.

6   It is suggested by Mr. Forbes that your consideration be given to the findings in this report.

You are correct if you . . .
1   Made "it is suggested" active
2   Used "you" as the second subject and "to consider" as the second verb

> *Mr. Forbes suggests* that *you consider* the findings in this report.

7   It was a matter of company policy which was the forcing factor in our action which resulted in a reduction of office staff.

You are correct if your sentence is active and if it has the same meaning as the original.

> Company *policy forced* us to reduce the office staff.

8   It was felt by both investigators that our questions would be answered by a single phone call.

You are correct if you . . .
1   Made "it was felt" active
2   Made "questions would be answered" active

> Both *investigators felt* that a single phone *call would answer* our questions.

9   Doyle's transistor lecture will be of interest to the whole research department once it has been edited by Murphy.

You are correct if you . . .
1   Made "lecture will be" active
2   Made "it has been edited" active

> Doyle's transistor *lecture will interest* the whole research department once *Murphy has edited* it.

10   Your check will be sent upon receipt of the enclosed form.

You are correct if you made "check will be sent" active.

We (I) will send your check when we (I) receive the enclosed form.

HELPFUL HINT

After you write the first draft of your next letter, make a mark in front of each active sentence. Then convert as many linking and passive sentences as you can to active sentences.

FIVE

BE SPECIFIC

In an age when so many are competing for attention and understanding, it is vitally important that business and industry learn to speak the language of their contemporaries. For we know that an institution endures and prospers largely because it can communicate with the people of its own time.

New York Life Insurance Company

Use your mask here.

1 As you have seen, effective writing depends on arranging your words in concise and forceful sentences. Clarity, in particular, depends on choosing words that will convey your exact meaning to your reader. Consider the following situation:

Suppose you are writing a thank-you note to someone who has written a letter of reference for you. Which is the better way to begin your letter?

A. Thanks for taking care of this matter for me.
B. Thanks for writing the letter of reference for me.

B (Sentence A may not communicate your exact meaning to your reader. He might know what matter you're referring to, but then again, he might have forgotten. The words "taking care of this matter" are too *general*; they will not effectively convey your exact meaning. Sentence B, however, leaves very little room for misunderstanding; it is *specific*.)

A CIRCLE OF MEANING

2a Think of a word as having a circle of meaning. A general word has a large circle. For instance, the circle of meaning for the verb "to travel" is large, encompassing such specific actions as walking, flying, or sailing. On the other hand, a specific word has a smaller circle of meaning. The specific verb "to crawl" stands for only one type of traveling action.

Look at this list:

A. symbol
B. exclamation point
C. punctuation mark

Does each of these contain within its circle of meaning the object, "!"? _____

Yes

2b Which stands for this object most exactly? _____

B

2c Which stands for this object next most exactly? _____

C ("Symbol" is the most general because it encompasses the other two within its circle of meaning.)

3a

A. insect
B. ant
C. living creature

Does each of the above words more or less describe the given object? _____

Yes

3b Which of the above describes the object most exactly? That is, which is most specific in this case? _____

B

3c Which is the next most specific? _____

A

4 "General" and "specific" are relative terms, so one can not always attach these labels with confidence. But in the following list, the distinction between specific and general words is fairly clear-cut. Write the letters of the specific words.

_____

A. effect
B. rye bread
C. idea
D. communication
E. Albuquerque
F. listen

G. use
H. sticky
I. very
J. great
K. sew
L. kick

B
E
F
H
K
L

5

A. silver certificate
B. dollar bill
C. unit of currency

Each of these items contains within its circle of meaning the object, $1. Which stands for this object most exactly? _____   Next most exactly? _____   Least exactly? _____

B
A
C

6 On the next page is a list of matched words. One of the words in each pair is more specific (has a more precise meaning) than the other. Copy the specific word from each pair.

course	physics
worthwhile	educational
morals	principles
to refund	to pay
to produce	to manufacture
to send	to deliver
zip code	number
pink	color
empty	hollow
better	more efficient

physics
educational
morals
to refund
to manufacture
to deliver
zip code
pink
hollow
more efficient

GENERAL vs. SPECIFIC WORDS

7 Both general and specific words have their place in business letters. But if you use general words when you want to convey a specific meaning, you reduce your chances of being clear to your reader. He may get the feeling that you have something to say to him but that you're not saying it.

For example, suppose you are the manager of an electrical power station, and your boss at the home office sends you a copy of the new safety regulations which he plans to implement at all stations. He asks you to review the proposed regulations and to criticize them. You find that regulation 6 will cause the oil-fired steam turbines, which run the dynamos, to consume oil inefficiently. You sit down to reply to your boss. Which of the following sentences will express your meaning better? _____

A. Certain aspects of inefficiency manifest themselves when we consider implementation of one of these regulations.
B. If we implement regulation 6, the turbines may consume as much as 10 percent more oil.

B (Your boss would learn next to nothing from sentence A. For instance, consider "aspects of inefficiency." These words are so general that they could refer to anything from an increase in oil consumption to increased time for hosiery inspection. And look at "manifest." This general action verb could mean that "aspects of inefficiency" will occur, or may occur, or may be imagined. And why beat around the bush with "one of these regulations" when one means regulation 6?

Granted, the writer of sentence A could write further sentences which would make his meaning clear, but that would indicate that he is not writing concisely and that the above sentence is not carrying its share of the communication load. Sentence B does the job clearly and concisely.)

8a As business writers, we want to communicate precise ideas, lucid arguments, and thoroughly defined concepts. Read the following:

Research results show that this procedure, if adopted, would have a measurable effect on production.

Two vague, general words make this sentence ineffective. What are they? _____

measurable effect

8b Does "measurable" tell you, really, how much effect the adoption of the procedure will have? _____

No (The effect could be very large or very small.)

8c And how about "effect"? Does this word give you much of an idea about the results which the adoption of the procedure will bring about? _____

No (It could be any result, from benefit to detriment.)

8d Use your own ideas in whatever context you wish and rewrite the last part of the above sentence to make it *specific.* _____

You are correct if the words you wrote are more informative than "measurable effect."

. . . would increase production by 50 percent.

or

. . . would greatly reduce production.

9a Examine the two examples below:

A. His report is not worthwhile.
B. His report doesn't give the information I asked for.

Which sentence is more meaningful? _____

B

9b "Worthwhile," as used above, is vague. Rewrite the following sentence so that it is more specific. _____

His lecture was very worthwhile.

Anything more specific than "worthwhile" is correct.

His lecture was *educational (witty, well prepared, thrilling, worth two hours of your time).*

10   Here's another vague usage.

I'll *contact* you next Thursday, April 15.

The reader has no idea how the writer is going to "contact" him. Rewrite the sentence to make it more specific. _____

Remember: your revision does not have to be worded exactly like ours. If you told the reader *how* you are going to "contact" him, you are correct.

I'll *phone* (*write, telegram*) you next Thursday, April 15.

11   Here's a phrase that is *both* wordy and vague.

Mr. Getty, we will decrease your monthly payment by $5 *in the foreseeable future.*

Mr. Getty wants to know exactly when he can expect his reduction. The writer could have eliminated the wordiness and vagueness of "in the foreseeable future" if he had supplied Mr. Getty with a _____

---

date, definite time (Sometimes, of course, it is not possible to give a date. If not, "next week" or "this month" would be better. If you must be vague, you can eliminate the wordiness of "in the foreseeable future" with "soon.")

12   In every sentence you write, try to be as specific as possible. This will make your sentences more concise and forceful. Copy the more specific word or phrase from the following examples. _____

Mrs. Shofner (came against/tripped on) (the doorsill/a low obstruction) as she (entered/was moving through the door of) the restaurant.

Mrs. Shofner *tripped* on the *doorsill* as she *entered* the restaurant.

13

I'm sure you will be able to find Miss VanLeunen's (whereabouts/address) in (a telephone book/an appropriate source of information). _____

I'm sure you will be able to find Miss VanLeunen's *address* in a *telephone book.*

14

We decided to abandon the warehouse (because of the following three factors/for the following three reasons). _____

We decided to abandon the warehouse for the following three *reasons.*

15

He is an expert in (his field/sand blasting). _____

He is an expert in *sand blasting.*

16   You've already learned about the advantages of using a specific action verb as the main verb of your sentence. For practice, choose the verb which most restricts the meaning of the following sentence.

A. influence
B. affect
C. prevent
D. tend to go against

This decision will _____ our employment of ten additional secretaries.

C

GENERAL WORDS HAVE THEIR USES

17 But does all this mean that effective business writers must exclude all general words from their letters?

Which of the following is a better answer to the above question? _____

A. Of course not. General words are useful and appropriate if they express what you mean. In other words, they will very effectively communicate a general thought.
B. Yes. Since all thoughts that are communicated in a business letter are specific, you should express them with specific words.

A (Although *most* of the ideas which you will have to express in business letters are specific and will be better expressed by specific words, we think A is the better answer, because no word is inherently ineffective. General words, if used wisely, will often express a general meaning effectively.)

18a Here's a situation:

Companies often receive requests for contributions. In this case, Reverend John Williams of the First Universal Church in Gramercy, Massachusetts, asked a nearby industrial plant to contribute to the church orphanage. Although the company has a sizable contributions budget, its policy allows donations to health and welfare organizations and to education, but not to religious organizations. The company doesn't want to mention this in its letter. Here's the turndown:

Dear Reverend Williams:

I'm sure you understand that during the year we receive hundreds of requests for help from worthy organizations like yours. We would, of course, like to support all these activities, but regretfully we are not able to contribute to your orphanage. I wish I could give you better news.

Sincerely yours,

Most of the words in this paragraph are (general/specific). _____

general

18b The thoughts which must be communicated to the reader are (general/specific). _____

general

18c Does the writer express exactly what he means to say? __ _____

Yes

18d   Do many business letters express thoughts of this kind? _____

No (In most business writing, you will not find many opportunities to use general words to express general ideas.)

19a   Surprisingly, you can often use specific words to express a general thought. Herbert Spencer, in his *Philosophy of Style*, demonstrated the advantages of using specific words by writing two paragraphs, one with general words and one with specific words.

A. In proportion as the manners, customs, and amusements of a nation are cruel and barbarous, the regulations of their penal code will be severe.	B. In proportion as men delight in battles, bull fights, and combats of gladiators, will they punish by hanging, burning, and the rack.

Do both paragraphs express essentially the same general thought?_____

Yes (Although they do not create the same image in the reader's mind, the generalized thought is exactly the same.)

19b   Which paragraph is more concise? _____

B

19c   Which paragraph has many more specific words? _____

B

19d   Which paragraph is more forceful, more interesting to read? _____

B (Most people like paragraph B better.)

20   Unfortunately we all tend to prefer general words because specific words are difficult to think of. And business writers are particularly apt to use them because they have much to write and little time. However, we hope that by this time you are convinced of the advantages of being specific and that you will take the time and make the additional effort.

Which of the following sentences is more difficult to write? _____

A.   If we may be of further service, please do not hesitate to call on us.
B.   If your faucet starts to leak again, call me, and I'll send our plumber free of charge.

B (Sentence A is such a general cliché that it has become almost meaningless. A writer certainly doesn't have to think very hard to produce it. And the reader is well aware of this. He is also aware that a writer has to think a little to come up with the specifics of sentence B and will probably be impressed more favorably.)

21   Business writers also tend to use general words because they face daily the task of writing letters which must meet similar situations and problems. Consequently, they accumulate a number of standard sentences which they think will do the job. These old standards are invariably general, all-purpose sentences, and a good many of them are clichés.

But think of your reader for a minute. He's an individual, and his situation, his problem, is always a little different from his fellow's. He appreciates it when a letter shows him that the writer has given him special consideration.

One way you can do this is to be specific, with words that apply to the reader's situation and his alone.

Which of the following sentences will demonstrate to the reader that he is receiving special attention from the writer? _____

    A. I notice on page nineteen of your proposal that you recommend a budget increase for the Bluestone Hospital. I think that . . .

    B. I have examined your proposal carefully. I think that . . .

A (Sentence B, the general one, is not too bad, but it will not convince the reader as well as the specific sentence. For when the reader sees the specific discussion of his proposal, he knows the writer has studied it carefully.)

Now begin the exercises.

EXERCISES

A Complete each sentence with the most *specific* word or phrase.

Use your mask here.

1 We will be happy to send you a check _____ .

    A. in due course
    B. as soon as possible
    C. by June 17

C

"I'm afraid you'll have to be a little more specific, Ma'am."

Drawing by C. Barsotti, © 1971, The New Yorker Magazine, Inc.

2 Mr. Depolo sells_____ .

   A. power packages
   B. car batteries
   C. electrical equipment

B

3 By playing fifty hoses systematically along the west fire line, the fire fighters _____ the progress of the blaze.

   A. checked
   B. inhibited
   C. successfully influenced

A

4 The court asked the taxpayer to _____ his taxes.

   A. pay
   B. arrange
   C. take care of

A

5 The agent _____ the bank reports.

   A. exposed himself to
   B. examined
   C. went over

B

6 The manager noticed that the lights were out, so he _____ that the workers had gone home.

   A. thought
   B. believed
   C. concluded

C

7 This _____ cost the company $11,000.

   A. incident
   B. unfortunate occurrence
   C. accident

C

8 The members of the panel proposed many _____ ideas.

   A. marvelous
   B. provocative
   C. worthwhile

B

9 On February 11, Preeble Industries _____ the Carlysle Estate.

   A. bought
   B. obtained
   C. acquired

   A

10 Please sign the application _____ .

   A. on the dotted line
   B. in the appropriate place
   C. near the bottom

   A

B Below is a list of specific words and a letter containing many inappropriate general words—in italics. Substitute the specific ones for the general ones.

On June 2,	order clerk
by June 30,	twenty dozen Pretzaleen slacks
mailed	for $5,826.58
invoice	phone

June 13,

Recently, one of my employees sent you our order for a *number of men's garments*. Unfortunately, we have not received shipment, although we have your *billing document* for the *purchase price*.

I would appreciate it if you would look into this and *contact* me *no later than the end of this month.*

June 13,

On June 2, my *order clerk mailed* you our order for *twenty dozen Pretzaleen slacks.* Unfortunately, we have not received shipment, although we have your *invoice for $5,826.58.*

I would appreciate it if you would look into this and *phone* me *by June 30* at the latest.

C This exercise may take as long as half an hour. So if you've been working more than an hour, take a break or save this exercise for another day.

Your title: Lawn and Shrubbery Consultant for the Green Vistas Outdoor Supply Company

Your job: answer the following letter.

Dear Sirs:

A whole lot of mushrooms are coming up on my lawn and just ruining it. It's been cool and damp lately. Is this what's causing all the trouble? What can I do to get rid of them?

Sincerely yours,
Mrs. Martha Towser

The specific facts at your fingertips:

1 Cool, damp weather encourages mushrooms.
2 Mushrooms are unsightly.
3 They won't hurt grass.
4 Raking the lawn cleans out existing mushrooms and reduces propagation by spores.
5 Raking the lawn also cleans away any accumulation of grass clippings which protect the mushrooms.
6 Green Vistas manufactures a can of fungicide called *Murder*.
7 It's available at all Green Vistas dealers.
8 Several customers have sprayed it on mushrooms with totally effective results.
9 You can't guarantee it will work on Towser's mushrooms.

Below is your first-draft letter. It's full of general and inflated words. Many of the sentences are passive or have being verbs. Rewrite the letter sentence by sentence so that it becomes clear, concise, and forceful. If you don't understand parts of the following letter, refer to the facts above to discover the missing meaning.

Dear Mrs. Towser:

1 You are correct in your assumption that the inclement weather is a cause of your trouble. 2 Although these growths are visually unpleasant, they have a neutral effect on your greenery.

3 There are several alternatives which may be taken:

A. 4 Free the premises of debris. 5 Thus the present growths will be eliminated and reproduction by the spores will be reduced. 6 An additional benefit of performing this action will be the elimination of other debris which may be a protective factor.

B. 7 Purchase an amount of our new chemical compound called *Murder*. 8 *Murder* is available in several convenient stores. 9 Several individuals have utilized it with a certain degree of effectiveness. 10 However, you should not take this as an assurance that this compound will have a measurable effect on your particular growths.

Sincerely yours,

Dear Mrs. Towser:

1 You're right, the cool, damp weather does encourage the mushrooms.

You should have . . .

1 Deflated and shortened "you are correct in your assumption that"
2 Used something more specific than "inclement"
3 Replaced the being verb with an action verb
4 Used "mushrooms" instead of "your trouble."

2 Although they are unsightly, they won't harm your grass (lawn).

You should have . . .

1 Deflated "visually unpleasant"
2 Replaced "have" with a more specific action verb
3 Used something more specific than "neutral effect" and "greenery."

3 Two remedies may help you get rid of your mushrooms:

You should have . . .

1 Replaced "are" with an action verb
2 Used something more specific than "several alternatives."

4 Rake the lawn.

You should have been more specific than "free the premises."

5 This will clean away your present mushrooms and reduce reproduction by the spores.

You should have . . .

1 Used something more specific than "growths"
2 Used "to eliminate" or a more specific action verb and "to reduce" as your main verbs.

6 Raking also cleans away any accumulation of grass clippings, which protect the mushrooms.

You should have . . .

1 Replaced the first being verb with an action verb
2 Replaced the second being verb with "to protect"
3 Replaced "factor" with "grass clippings."

7 Buy a can of our new fungicide, *Murder.*

You should have . . .

1 Deflated "purchase"
2 Been more specific than "an amount of"
3 Been more specific than "chemical compound."

8 *Murder* is available at your nearest Green Vistas dealer.

You should have used something more specific than "several convenient stores."

9 Several customers have sprayed it on mushrooms with totally effective results.

You should have . . .

1 Been more specific than "individuals"
2 Deflated "utilized" or replaced it with a more specific action verb
3 Been more specific than "a certain degree of effectiveness."

10 However, I can't guarantee that *Murder* will entirely eliminate your mushrooms.

You should have . . .

1 Replaced "should not take" with a more specific action verb
2 Been more specific than "assurance"
3 Been more specific than "this compound"
4 Been more specific than "measurable effect"
5 Been more specific than "growths."

Your revised letter should now read something like this:

Dear Mrs. Towser:

You're right, the cool, damp weather does encourage mushrooms. Although they are unsightly, they won't harm your lawn.

Two remedies may help you get rid of your mushrooms:

1   Rake the lawn. This will clean away your present mushrooms and reduce reproduction by spores. Raking also cleans away any accumulation of grass clippings, which protect the mushrooms.
2   Buy a can of our new fungicide, *Murder*, which is available at your nearest Green Vistas dealer.

Although I can't guarantee that *Murder* will entirely eliminate your mushrooms, several customers have used it with totally effective results.

Sincerely,

HELPFUL HINT

After you write your next business letter, set it aside for a while. Then pretend that you are the reader who has just received the letter. Read it slowly. Are there any words that are too general? That is, would they puzzle someone who does not know what you are trying to get across? If so, replace the general words with more specific ones.

SIX
BE SIMPLE TO BE CONCISE

If what you write is not clear, the reader will not know what you want him to do. If you are confused or wordy, the reader will waste time figuring out what you mean or will have to go back to ask you for a clarification. Improving your writing can enhance your reputation as a thinker and as a leader.

Writing Guide for Naval Officers, United States Navy

Use your mask here.

INFLATED LANGUAGE

1 One of the main causes of wordy, unclear writing is the use of *inflated* words instead of *simple* ones. For instance, some writers take a simple word like "best" and dress it up so that it becomes "optimum." Inflated words like this have the same meaning but are fancier, less familiar, and consequently, more difficult to read. Look at this sentence:

> It was difficult to determine clearly what motivational factors caused his action. (Twelve words)

The meaning of this sentence is fairly clear, yet it is slow in getting across to us. The words are unnecessarily elaborate and the sentence is wordy.

To deflate a sentence, it's often helpful to think of how you would express the thought if you were talking to someone. Rewrite the above sentence using the short simple words you would say to someone in the office. _____

Your answer is correct if it is less high-flown than the original.

> It was hard to tell why he did it. (Nine words, a saving of three)

2 Avoiding inflated language requires a letter writer to be honest with himself and his reader. For all of us tend sometimes to write more formally than we should. For instance, a writer may say, "An investigation of such pertinent information as happened to be immediately available . . ." when he really means, "I checked my notes." In this case, "an investigation" suggests a formal action, which is not strictly true. By using inflated words in place of simple ones, the writer has not actually lied, but he has hinted at more than is literally true.

Most of us tend to use the long, inflated word in place of its short, simple brother because many of the ideas we must express in business *are* simple. We try to hide this simplicity because we don't want the reader to think *we* are simple.

And so, "done again" becomes "determined to repeat." "We operate" becomes "we are at the present time engaged in operating." And "borrow" becomes 'procure on a loan basis."

But we all might as well face up to the awful truth:

> The obvious is better than obvious avoidance of it.
>
> H. W. Fowler

Which of the following better expresses the sentiment here?

> A. The conviction that profundity of thought is evidenced by complexity of vocabulary is erroneous.
> B. Big words don't impress nobody.

Answer B is correct, grammar notwithstanding.

3 Here's a good principle:

> Deflate inflated words.

The beauty of simple writing is that it is usually so much more *concise*. Examine the following:

> Our activities must be commensurate with the actual budgetary situation, particularly with regard to the need to decrease monetary expenditures. (Twenty words)

Deflate this inflated sentence and thus shorten it.

Use your own judgment. Did you deflate everything that can be deflated? If you did, you are correct.

> Decrease spending to fit the budget. (Six words, a saving of fourteen)
>
> or
>
> We should keep costs within the budget. (Seven words, a saving of thirteen)

4   George Orwell (the author of *Animal Farm* and *1984*) once wrote an article criticizing government writing in England. At one point, he attacked the bureaucratic habit of using inflated, pompous language. To illustrate his point, he translated a passage from the Bible into government jargon.

BIBLE PASSAGE	ORWELL'S SATIRE
I returned, and saw under the sun, that the race is not to the swift, nor the battle to the strong, neither yet riches to men of understanding, nor yet favor to men of skill, but time and chance happenth to all.	Objective consideration of contemporary phenomena compels the conclusion that success or failure in competitive activities exhibits no tendency to be commensurate with innate capacity, but that a considerable element of the unpredictable must inevitably be taken into account.

Notice that Orwell's satire has many general and inflated words while the Bible passage has many simple, specific words. We need not point out how much more effective the Bible passage is.

> I recommended that he strive to conduct himself in a way more conducive to earlier arrival at the office lest the need for official action arise. (Twenty-six words)

Is this the way you would say it if you were speaking to someone? Rewrite it.

> I told him to get to work on time or I would have to take action. (Sixteen words, a saving of ten)

5a   Two words may have exactly the same meaning, yet one may be long and complicated, while the other is short and simple:

> A.   to effectuate
> B.   to effect

Do these two verbs have the same meaning? _____

Yes

5b Which is the simple verb?_____

B

6 Which of the following is inflated? _____

   A. motive
   B. motivational factor

B

7 Which is the simple verb below? _____

   A. to utilize
   B. to use

B

8 Which one is inflated? _____

   A. enclosed
   B. attached herewith

B

9 Which one is inflated?_____

   A. inasmuch as
   B. since

A

WORDY OR UNNECESSARY PHRASES

10 Wordy or unnecessary phrases are often inflated and can usually be shortened. Look at the following sentence:

We will remove in the neighborhood of about 100,000 cubic yards of earth. (Thirteen words)

Test this sentence for wordy or unnecessary phrases. If you find any, rewrite it.

_____

We will remove *about* 100,000 cubic yards of earth. (Nine words, a saving of four)

11 Deflate and shorten this sentence. _____

We will cooperate to the fullest extent of our ability. (Ten words)

You are correct if you eliminated "extent of our ability."

We will cooperate *fully (completely, totally, etc.).* (Four words, a saving of six)

or

We will help as much as possible. (Seven words, a saving of three)

12 Shorten this sentence. _____

I hope to hear from you at the earliest practicable date. (Eleven words)

If you used "contact," you are incorrect.

I hope to hear from you (very) *soon (early)*. (Seven words, a saving of four)

13   Shorten this sentence. _____

We realize that this is information of a confidential nature. (Ten words)

We realize that this information is confidential. (Seven words, a saving of three)

or

We realize that this is confidential information. (Seven words, a saving of three)

14   This sentence has two doublets. Write it concisely. _____

I look forward with anticipation to our mutual cooperation on Project Sampson.

The two doublets are: "look forward with anticipation," and "mutual cooperation."

I look forward to *cooperating* with you on Project Sampson. (Ten words, a saving of two)

15   Always be on the alert for ideas which at first glance seem all right, but which, on careful consideration, are not really necessary.

The secretaries went through the papers and separated them into three piles. (Twelve words)

There is an unnecessary idea here. Rewrite to eliminate it. _____

The secretaries separated the papers into three piles. (Eight words, a saving of four. The secretaries would have to go through the papers to separate them.)

16   Rewrite this by getting rid of the unnecessary idea. _____

According to our records, we find that you have already paid the March interest.

We find that you have paid the interest for March. (Ten words, a saving of four)

or

Our records show that you paid the interest for March. (Ten words, a saving of four)

"THE (NOUN) OF" PHRASES

17   Phrases like "the improvement of" and "the establishment of" usually can be compressed to participles like "improv*ing*" and "establish*ing*" or to infinitives like "*to* improve" and "*to* establish." Thus, a "the (noun) of" phrase almost always indicates wordiness and a lack of force.

We are interested in the construction of a match factory. (Ten words)

Shorten it. _____

We are interested in *constructing* a match factory. (Eight words, a saving of two)

18 Rewrite the following, using the infinitive form instead of the "the (noun) of" phrase. _____

We intend the undertaking of special studies. (Seven words)

We intend *to undertake* special studies. (Six words, a saving of one. Note how much more forceful the infinitive is.)

UNNECESSARY CLAUSES

19 Here is a *new* principle for saving words:

Be *stingy* with modifying clauses.

Examine the clause below:

You will be required to fill out forms *which are detailed and lengthy*. (Thirteen words)

Two words can be removed by turning the contents of the "which" clause (the modifying clause) into adjectives.

You will be required to fill out _____ and _____ forms. (Eleven words, a saving of two)

detailed and lengthy

20 Here's another sentence with a clause modifier.

This was a decision which was difficult for us to make. (Eleven words)

Rewrite this sentence to make it more concise. _____

You are correct if you changed the "which" clause and your sentence is less than eleven words.

We made this *difficult* decision. (Five words, a saving of six)

or

This was a *difficult* decision for us (to make). (Seven words, a saving of four)

21 Rewrite this sentence by changing the modifying clause to a phrase. _____

Mr. Lawrence Ross, *who* is our local representative, will call you. (Eleven words)

Mr. Lawrence Ross, *our local representative*, will call you. (Nine words, a saving of two)

22 Compress this sentence by getting rid of the two unnecessary modifying clauses.

While Mr. Harry Sampson, who is our London sales manager, was in New York on vacation, he attended our annual meeting which was held in the Waldorf-Astoria Hotel. (Twenty-eight words)

While Mr. Harry Sampson, *our London sales manager*, was in New York on vacation, he attended our annual meeting *at* the Waldorf-Astoria Hotel. (Twenty-three words, a saving of five)

23 Rewrite this to eliminate the subject of the clause. _____

Files wnich are left in the old office should be carefully marked. (Twelve words)

Files left in the old office should be carefully marked. (Ten words, a saving of two)

24 Shorten this. _____ _

Reports which are important should be saved.

Important reports should be saved.

25 Shorten this. _____

Men who have great strength are in demand.

Very strong men are in demand.

26 Shorten this. _____

This service, which is offered without charge, is available here.

This service, offered without charge, is available here.

or

This free service is available here.

27 Generally, some modifying clauses are wordy. However, for emphasis, you may sometimes want to keep the clause modifier. Which of the following gives *more* emphasis to the taxpayer's delinquency?_____

    A. This delinquent taxpayer asks that . . .
    B. This taxpayer, who is delinquent, asks that . . .

    B

    You can see, then, that there are many ways to save words. You can . . .

1 deflate inflated language
2 compress or cut wordy or unnecessary phrases
3 convert "the (noun) of" phrases to participles or infinitives
4 be stingy with clauses

We have it before us, its contents noted,
That your letter arrived of recent date:
We have it before us, its contents noted,
Herewith enclosed are the prices we quoted.
Attached please find, as per your request,
The samples you wanted, and we would suggest
Regarding the matter and due to the fact
That up to this moment your order we've lacked,
We hope you will not delay it unduly
And we beg to remain Yours very truly.

Anonymous

Now begin the exercises.

EXERCISES

A Match the simple, short word with the inflated word which has exactly the same meaning.

Use your mask here.

INFLATED		SIMPLE	
1 Approximately	_____	A.	Finish
2 Subsequently	_____	B.	Repeat
3 Anticipated	_____	C.	Best
4 Causative factor	_____	D.	Copy
5 Optimum	_____	E.	Begin
6 Inaugurate	_____	F.	About
7 Finalize	_____	G.	Cause
8 Manifest	_____	H.	Expected
9 Replicate	_____	I.	Show
10 Recapitulate	_____	J.	Later

1 F
2 J
3 H
4 G
5 C
6 E
7 A
8 I
9 D
10 B

B Rewrite these inflated sentences with shorter, simpler words.

1 I want to congratulate you on the occasion of your merger with Psychoprobe, Inc.

Congratulations on your merger with Psychoprobe, Inc.

2 We then carried out your orders without further delay.

We then carried out your orders *immediately.*

3 I have your letter under date of August 13.

I have your letter *of (dated)* August 13.

4 I hope this is agreeable to your wishes on this matter.

I hope this *is what you want.*

or

I hope this *is satisfactory (agreeable)* to you.

or

I hope this *suits* (*pleases*) you.

5 We must plan with a view to cutting the budget.

We must plan *to cut* the budget.

6 Will you be kind enough to send these forms to us?

(Would you) *please* send us these forms. (?)

7 In this day and age, competition is much keener.

Today (*these days*), competition is much keener.

C Make the following sentences more concise.

  1 We wish to aid and abet our customers by helping them with their difficult problems which they have when they shop. (Twenty-one words)

___

You should have . . .

1 Corrected the doublet, "aid and abet"
2 Converted the clause, "which they have when they shop," into the adjective "shopping"

We want *to help* our customers with their difficult *shopping* problems. (Eleven words)

  2 You will undoubtedly be interested to know that it has come to our attention through channels that we are unable to divulge because they are confidential, that a rival photography shop will be opened close to yours. (Thirty-seven words)

___

You should have . . .

1 Eliminated "you will undoubtedly be interested to know that"
2 Used an action verb in place of "has come"
3 Converted "that we are unable to divulge because they are confidential" to the adjective "confidential"
4 Made "shop will be opened" active

We have discovered, through confidential channels, that a rival (photography) shop will open near yours. (Fourteen words)

  3 The situation is, in my judgment, if I may express a personal opinion, dangerous to our plan for expansion within the next year. (Twenty-three words)

___

You should have . . .

1 Replaced "is" with an action verb
2 Written an active sentence
3 Changed "in my judgment, if I may express a personal opinion" to "I think" or "in my opinion"
4 Eliminated "within the"

I think that the situation endangers our plan for expansion next year. (Twelve words)

4   The responsibility of our production department is to see that it meets the requirements of our sales division. (Eighteen words)

Our production department must meet the requirements of our sales division. (Eleven words)

or

Our production department is responsible for meeting the requirements of our sales division. (Thirteen words)

Although the above sentence has a being verb, it is an acceptable revision.

5   Trusting that this is what you want, your policy was endorsed, as requested by you. (Fifteen words)

You should have . . .

1   Eliminated "trusting that this is what you want"
2   Made "policy was endorsed" active
3   Made "requested by you" active

We (I) have endorsed your policy as you asked. (Eight words)

6   If you are interested in the course of procedure outlined above, . . . (Eleven words)

You should have compressed "course of procedure outlined above."

If you are interested in this (the above) procedure, . . . (Seven words)

or

If the above procedure interests you, . . . (Six words)

or

If you want to do this, . . . (Six words)

7   As soon as we are in receipt of this information from them, it will be sent to you. (Eighteen words)

You should have . . .

1   Replaced "are" with "to receive"
2   Made *both* subject-verbs active

As soon as *we receive* this information, *we will send* it to you. (Thirteen words)

8   You will be pleased with this clock which is dependable and attractive. (Twelve words)

You should have done away with the "which" clause.

You will be pleased with (will like) this dependable and attractive clock. (Ten words)

or

This dependable and attractive clock will please you. (Eight words)

9 I regret to say that, in the best interests of all concerned, the delay of your admission to the Inner Sanctum Country Club would be advisable for the present. (Twenty-nine words)

You should have . . .

1 Changed "I regret to say that" to "I am sorry that"
2 Eliminated "in the best interests of all concerned"
3 Used a specific action verb in place of "would be advisable"
4 Eliminated "for the present" if "to delay" was your main verb

I am sorry that we must delay your admission to the Inner Sanctum Country Club. (Fifteen words)

10 These reports, which are both specific and comprehensive, should be sent to the foreign office. (Fifteen words)

You should have done away with the "which" clause.

These specific and comprehensive reports should be sent to the foreign office. (Twelve words)

11 The improvement of the distribution system will result from the establishment of efficient delivery methods. (Fifteen words)

You should have . . .

1 Used "to improve" as the main verb
2 Made the sentence active

(Establishing) Efficient delivery methods will improve the distribution system (Eight words)

12 If in the future you feel that we can be of further service, do not hesitate to contact us. (Nineteen words)

You should have . . .

1 Eliminated "in the future"
2 Used an action verb in place of "can be"
3 Made all subject-verbs active

If we can do anything more to help you, let us know. (Twelve words)

or

If you need more help, please write. (Seven words)

HELPFUL HINT

When you review your first-draft letter next time, set a goal for yourself. Say to yourself, "I'm going to cut at least ten words from this letter." Then see if you can do it without losing clarity or courtesy.

"I hate people who use big words when little ones will do the job."

Drawing by D. Fradon, © 1970, The New Yorker Magazine, Inc.

SEVEN
USE MODIFIERS CLEARLY

There is no greater problem in the business world than that of effectively presenting thoughts and ideas. I believe that the student who learns to communicate effectively through speech and writing will make himself more valuable in whatever work he selects.

Frederic N. Schwartz, Chairman of the Executive Committee, Bristol-Myers Company

Use your mask here.

SINGLE-WORD MODIFIERS

1a   Previous chapters have been primarily concerned with writing sentences which have an effective main statement (subject-verb). In this chapter, however, we will be dealing with the problem of expressing ideas clearly by using modifiers effectively.

Let's review what a modifier is. Basically, it's any word or group of words that describes or qualifies another word or group of words. Let's start with *single-word modifiers*.

He quickly analyzes new data.

You can see that the main statement of this sentence is "He . . . analyzes . . . data." The other words in the statement either describe or qualify certain words of the main statement. For example, because "quickly" describes the action of the sentence, it modifies what word? _____

---

analyzes

1b   What is the other single-word modifier in the above sentence? _____

---

new

1c   What is the word it modifies? _____

---

data

2a   What is the bare main statement of this sentence? _____

Our office handles incoming mail efficiently.

. . . office handles . . . mail . . .

2b   List the first single-word modifier and the word it modifies. _____

---

our   ———————▶   office

2c   There are two other single-word modifiers in the above sentence. List them along with the word each modifies. _____

---

incoming   ———————▶   mail
efficiently   ———————▶   handles

PHRASE MODIFIERS

3a   In addition to the single-word modifier, consider the phrase modifier:

He put the books *in the office.*

What is the bare main statement? _____

He put . . . books . . .

3b   "In the office" qualifies the action by telling us where the books were placed. In other words, this phrase modifies the word _____.

---

put

4a   What is the bare main statement of the following? _____

Workers on the top floor clean tanks of various sizes.

Workers . . . clean tanks . . .

4b List the single-word modifiers and the word each modifies. Don't bother to list articles such as "the" or "a."

top ——————→ floor
various ——————→ sizes

4c List the two phrase-modifiers and the words that each modifies. _____

on the top floor ——————→ workers
of various sizes ——————→ tanks

CLAUSE MODIFIERS

5a Besides single-word and phrase modifiers, we have the clause modifier:

The retailers in the showroom can obtain free products *which sell rapidly*.

What is the bare main statement of the sentence? _____

. . . retailers . . . can obtain . . . products

5b Notice that the modifying clause has a subject and verb of its own. What is its subject? _____

which

5c The verb of the clause is _____ .

sell

5d What is the word that the clause modifies? _____

products

5e There is a single-word modifier in the *clause*. List it and the word it modifies.

rapidly ——————→ sell

5f There is also a phrase modifier in the sentence. List it and the word it modifies. _____

in the showroom ——————→ retailers

6a What is the bare main statement of the following sentence? _____

Most people who have high incomes are potential investors in preferred stock.

. . . people . . . are . . . investors . . .

6b Try listing all the *single-word modifiers* and the word each modifies. _____

Most ——————→ people
high ——————→ incomes
potential ——————→ investors
preferred ——————→ stock

6c Now list the *phrase modifier* and the word it modifies. _____

in preferred stock ————————→ investors

6d What is the *clause modifier* and the word it modifies? _____

who have high incomes ————————→ people

7a What is the bare main statement below? _____

After you write the first draft of your letter, the supervisor will criticize it.

. . . supervisor will criticize it.

7b List the phrase modifier and the word it modifies. _____

of your letter ————————→ draft

7c List the clause modifier and the word it modifies. _____

After you write the first draft of your letter ————————→ will criticize

MISPLACED MODIFIERS

8a Now that we have reviewed the different kinds of modifiers, let's talk about misplaced modifiers. Sometimes a misplaced modifier can be humorous, as in this sentence quoted by *The New Yorker* magazine from a novel:

Whatever her thoughts, they were interrupted as the hotel door opened and a young woman carrying a baby and her husband entered.

The British also are not immune to the misplaced modifier, as in the following specimen from Sir Ernest Gower's book, *The Complete Plain Words*:

There was a discussion yesterday on the worrying of sheep by dogs in the Minister's room.

However, most misplaced modifiers are either dull or unclear. They annoy the reader and embarrass the writer. Examine this sentence.

No security regulations shall be distributed to personnel that are out of date.

Does this sentence say what the writer means? _____

No (The writer didn't mean to say that the *personnel* are out of date.)

8b The above sentence has two interpretations (is ambiguous) because the clause modifier, "that are out of date," is misplaced. "That are out of date" is too close to "personnel." For clarity, the clause modifier should be placed near the word

_____ .

regulations

8c Make the above sentence clear by placing the clause near the word it modifies.

_____

No security regulations *that are out of date* shall be distributed to personnel.

9a Single-word modifiers such as "only" can be placed almost anywhere in a sentence, and so are likely to be misplaced. Look at this sentence. _____

The actuary *only* can solve the problem.

Could this sentence mean that the actuary is the only individual capable of solving the problem?_____

Yes

9b Could this sentence also mean that the only thing this actuary can do is solve the problem? _____

Yes

9c The above sentence is ambiguous (has two interpretations) because "only" is placed so that it can modify either "actuary" or "can solve." Rewrite the sentence so that it can only have the *first* interpretation. _____

Only the actuary can solve the problem.

9d Rewrite the sentence so that it can only have the *second* interpretation.

_____

The actuary can *only* solve the problem.

10a The client decided also to cancel the contract on Thursday.

Can this mean that there were several things that the client *decided* to do on Thursday, among which was the cancellation of the contract? _____

Yes

10b Can this also mean that there were several things that the client *canceled* on Thursday, among which was the contract? _____

Yes

10c The above sentence is ambiguous because "also" is placed near words that it might reasonably modify. They are "decided" and "cancel." Move the modifier so that the sentence has the interpretation in 10*a* only. _____

The client *also* decided to cancel the contract on Thursday.

11a Modifying *phrases* can also wander.

We need a man to watch the house with police experience.

Does this sentence say what the writer means? _____

No

11b What is the modifying phrase that has wandered away from the word it should modify? _____

---

with police experience

11c What word should this phrase modify? _____

---

man

11d Rewrite the sentence by placing the phrase next to the word it modifies.

_____

We need a man *with police experience* to watch the house.

12a   Here's another problem.

Several new cases have been closed by agents that are under four years old.

What kind of modifier has been misplaced here? A clause, a phrase, or a single-word? _____

_____

a clause

12b   What is the word this clause should modify? _____

_____

cases

12c   Rewrite the sentence with the modifier in the right place. _____

_____

Several new cases *that are under four years old* have been closed by agents.

13a   Mr. Tyler agreed after he landed the contract to give his men a pay raise.

Could this sentence mean that Mr. Tyler did his agreeing after he had in fact landed the contract?_____

_____

Yes

13b   Could this sentence also mean that Mr. Tyler did his agreeing before he landed the contract and that he said he would give his mean a raise after he did?_____

_____

Yes

13c   Because the above sentence has these two interpretations, it is ambiguous. What is the clause or phrase that has been misplaced?_____

_____

after he landed the contract

13d   The above sentence is ambiguous because the clause modifier is placed near two words it might reasonably modify. The two words are _____ and

_____ .

_____

agreed
(to) give

13e   Move the modifier so that the sentence has only the interpretation in 13*a*.

_____

_____

After he landed the contract, Mr. Tyler agreed to give his men a pay raise.
                                          or
Mr. Tyler, *after he landed the contract,* agreed to give his men a pay raise.

13f   Move the modifier so that the sentence has only the interpretation in 13*b*.

_____

Mr. Tyler agreed to give his men a pay raise *after he landed the contract.*

14a   What words are misplaced below? _____

This speaker should be instructed more carefully to discuss the topic.

_____

more carefully

14b   Write *two* unambiguous versions of the above sentence. _____

This speaker should be *more carefully* instructed to discuss the topic.

and

This speaker should be instructed to discuss the topic *more carefully*.

DANGLING MODIFIERS

15 Sometimes a writer places a modifier in a sentence and forgets to provide it with anything to modify. The modifier is then forced to try to hang on to the nearest or handiest word regardless of whether it can logically do so. When this occurs, modifiers are said to *dangle.*

To obtain these books, this form must be signed.

"To obtain these books" is near "form," but it cannot logically modify it, since the form cannot take action by itself. Infinitives have a special tendency to dangle.

Rewrite this sentence. Change the main statement by including a new subject that can be modified by "to obtain these books." _____

You are correct if the subject of your revision is something that can obtain books.

To obtain these books, you (they, Mr. Jones, etc.) must sign this form. (Notice that "to obtain these books" no longer dangles; it logically modifies "you.")

16a Does the sentence below say what the writer means? _____

After eating our lunch, the bus departed.

No

16b The phrase in the above sentence is called a participle. Because it has nothing to logically modify, it is a dangling participle. Rewrite the sentence by changing the subject of the main statement. This new subject should be something that is capable of "eating our lunch." _____

You are correct if the subject of your revision can be logically modified by the participle.

After eating our lunch, *we* (they, Mr. Jones, etc.) departed in the bus.

16c You can also rewrite the original sentence by changing the phrase to a clause. Give it a subject and verb of its own. _____

After we (they, etc.) ate our lunch, the bus departed.

or

The bus departed after we (they, etc.) ate our lunch.

16d Now compare your two revisions. Do they have exactly the same meaning?

No (Since the original sentence has several interpretations, it is not only ridiculous but ambiguous.)

17a Rewrite the following sentence by changing the participle to a clause.

Knowing that you want it right away, your medicine is being sent by air mail.

_____

Since I (we, they, etc.) know that you want your medicine right away, it is being sent by air mail.

or

Since I (we, they, etc.) know that you want it right away, your medicine is being sent by air mail.

17b Now rewrite the sentence by changing the subject of the main statement.

_____

Knowing that you want your medicine right away, *I (we, they, etc.) sent it by air mail*.

or

Knowing that you want it right away, *I (we, they, etc.) sent your medicine by air mail*.

18 Give *two* effective revisions of this sentence. _____

Having paid your annual premium last July, there will be no further payment until July of next year.

You are correct if you changed the participle to a clause in one revision and if you changed the subject of the main statement in the other.

Since you paid your annual premium last July, there will be no further payment until July of next year.

and

Having paid your annual premium last July, *you* will not have to pay another until July of next year.

Now begin the exercises.

EXERCISES

A The following sentences are not clear either because the modifiers are misplaced or because they dangle. Rewrite them.

Use your mask here.

1 Read on, and you will find out how to beat the stock market in a minute.

You are correct if you moved "in a minute" closer to "will find."

> Read on, and you will find out *in a minute* how to beat the stock market.
>
> or
>
> Read on, and *in a minute* you will find out how to beat the stock market.

2 To improve this report, more data must be accumulated.

You are correct if you changed the dangling infinitive to a clause or if you changed the subject of the main statement so that the participle can logically modify it.

> *If you are going to improve this report*, more data must be accumulated (if you are going to improve this report).
>
> or
>
> To improve this report, *you (we, they, Mr. Jones, etc.)* must accumulate more data (to improve this report).

3 The district attorney decided after the meeting to begin the investigation.

There are two interpretations of the above sentence. Give both.

You are correct if "after the meeting" clearly modifies "decided" in one revision and clearly modifies "to begin" in the other.

> *After the meeting*, the district attorney decided to begin the investigation.
>
> and
>
> The district attorney decided to begin the investigation *after the meeting*.

4 Rushing to meet the project deadline, many errors were made.

You are correct if you changed the dangling participle to a clause or if you changed the subject of the main statement so that the participle can logically modify it.

> *Because we (I, they, he, etc.) rushed to meet the project deadline*, we made many errors.
>
> or
>
> Rushing to meet the project deadline, *we (I, they, he, etc.)* made many errors.

5 The annual dinner will be held in the ballroom of the hotel consisting of the regular banquet fare.

You are correct if the phrase "consisting of the regular banquet fare" is closer to "dinner."

> The annual dinner, *consisting of the regular banquet fare*, will be held in the ballroom of the hotel.

6 We have examined the report you sent in great detail.

You are correct if "in great detail" clearly modifies "have examined."

We have examined *in great detail* the report you sent.

7 I recommend him as an employee without qualification.

You are correct if "without qualification" clearly modifies "recommend."

Without qualification, I recommend (without qualification) him as an employee.

8 He almost earns $100 a week.

You are correct if "almost" clearly modifies "$100."

He earns *almost* $100 a week.

9 The man had an appointment waiting in my office.

You are correct if "waiting in my office" clearly modifies "man."

The man *waiting in my office* had an appointment.

10 The executives decided before the meeting to report to the president.
Give both interpretations.

You are correct if "before the meeting" clearly modifies "decided" in one revision and clearly modifies "to report" in the other.

Before the meeting, the executives decided to report to the president. (This means that the executives decided to report before the meeting. However, exactly *when* they would report is not given.)

and

The executives decided to report to the president *before the meeting*. (This means that the executives also decided *when* to report. They would report *before* the meeting.)

HELPFUL HINT

Go through the first draft of the next letter you write and test all your modifiers. Make sure that each one is as close as possible to the word it modifies. Be especially careful to check whether your infinitives and participles dangle.

EIGHT
GIVE YOUR IDEAS
PROPER EMPHASIS

Not until you have learned to select almost
unconsciously the central, dominating thought of your
sentence, and to group around this in varying degrees of
emphasis the secondary or modifying thoughts, have you
learned to think clearly.

David Lambuth

Use your mask here.

LACK OF SUBORDINATION

1 The last chapter was primarily concerned with the mechanics of writing with modifiers. You learned to place them as close as possible to the words they modify and to detect and correct dangling modifiers. In this chapter, you will learn some new techniques which will help you use modifiers to give proper emphasis to your ideas.

Examine the examples below:

A. To bring existing statistics up to date, we will begin in June a survey of truck transportation.

B. We want to bring existing statistics up to date. To do this, we will begin a survey of truck transportation. June will be the starting time.

Both of these examples are clear, and none of the modifiers are misplaced or dangle. Yet one is more forceful and concise. Also it seems to have a better balance between ideas. Which one? _____

A [In example A, the most important idea is properly expressed by the subject-verb-object (the words of the main statement), while the secondary ideas are expressed in modifiers. In B, however, all the ideas have been given equal rank. That is, each has been expressed in a main statement, thus creating a choppy, disjointed effect. This fault is caused by *lack of subordination.*]

2 One of the marks of a mature business-letter writer is his ability to give his ideas proper emphasis. You can do this by following this principle:

Express your ideas in forms which truly reflect their importance.

Basically, there can be four types or forms within a sentence:

A. The words of the main statement (subject-verb-object)
B. Clause modifiers
C. Phrase modifiers
D. Single-word modifiers

Which of these four forms would you choose if you wished to give the *most* emphasis to a particular idea? _____ The least? _____

A
D

3a Let's consider an example of how the same idea can be expressed in different forms.

Mr. Peterson is competent, and he will be ready to begin work within two weeks.

The two basic ideas of this sentence concern Mr. Peterson's competence and his availability. Are these two ideas expressed in the same types of forms? _____

Yes

3b In the preceding, each idea is given the same emphasis because each is expressed in the same type of form—a main statement. But suppose that for some reason, the writer wanted to emphasize the importance of Mr. Peterson's availability rather than his competence. He could then *subordinate* the competence idea as follows:

Mr. Peterson, *who is competent*, will be ready to begin work within two weeks.

In this case, the idea concerning Mr. Peterson's competence has been expressed in what type of form? —————

———

a clause modifier

3c Now suppose that the writer wanted to give even less emphasis to the idea concerning Mr. Peterson's competence. He could do so in the following manner:

Competent Mr. Peterson will be ready to begin work within two weeks.

What type of form has now been used to express the idea of Mr. Peterson's competence? —————

———

a single-word modifier

4a Thus, the same idea can be expressed in a main statement, a clause modifer, a phrase modifier, or a single-word modifer—in descending degree of emphasis. Normally, you won't be concerned with the problem of giving emphasis to your ideas while you write your first draft. However, when you revise it, you may often find that you have chosen a form which gives too much or too little emphasis to an idea. If so, you should express that idea in a form which more nearly reflects its importance.

Examine this sentence:

Next to the main building, there is a lot in which students should park their cars.

What is the bare main statement of this sentence? —————

———

. . there is a lot . . .

4b Compare the thought expressed in the main statement with the thought in the "which" clause. Which is more important? The thought in the clause or the main statement? —————

———

the clause

4c Rewrite the sentence so that the main idea is expressed by the main statement.

—————

———

Students should park their cars in the lot next to the main building.

5a Even when your main statement expresses your main idea, your secondary ideas may be expressed by the wrong modifying form and given *too much* importance.

We found the missing documents, which were located under a pile of newspapers.

What is the bare main statement? —————

We found . . . documents . . .

5b Notice the idea expressed in the "which" clause. Assume that it really doesn't need that much attention. Rewrite the sentence by reducing the clause to a phrase.

We found the missing documents *under a pile of newspapers.*

6a Sometimes even a phrase needs to be reduced to a single word. Here's an example that has unnecessary phrases:

Yesterday, the manufacturing vice president announced a new regulation for the safety of workers on the assembly line.

How many phrases follow the word "regulation"? _____

three (1. *for the safety* 2. *of workers* 3. *on the assembly line.*)

6b Two of these phrases are unnecessary. Reduce them to single words and rewrite the sentence. _____

Yesterday, the manufacturing vice president announced a new *safety* regulation for *assembly-line* workers.

7 Consider this example:

Auto production and sales increased sharply last November, and this occurred particularly in the Detroit area.

Notice that we have *two* main statements connected by "and." But let's assume the second idea does not deserve the importance of a main statement. Reduce the second idea to a phrase and rewrite the sentence. _____

Auto production and sales, *particularly in the Detroit area*, increased sharply last November (particularly in the Detroit area).

TOO MUCH SUBORDINATION

8 In the previous examples, you have seen that some ideas are given *more* importance than they deserve. Occasionally, you will choose forms that give your ideas *less* importance than they deserve. Consider this sentence:

Please return the signed contract to us by December 15.

Let's say that, in the past, the reader has overlooked the idea that the contract must be signed. The writer can now give this idea more emphasis by expressing it in a clause rather than a single-word modifier. Rewrite the sentence giving this idea more importance.

Please return the contract, *which you must sign*, to us by December 15. (Another way to stress the importance of the "signing" idea is to make it part of the main statement: "Please *sign* and return the contract to us by December 15.")

9   Here's a more extreme example of oversubordination.

> One of our golden retriever two-month-old pups from Ardmor Kennels' regis-tered champion stock would make an ideal Christmas gift for your son or daughter with papers and all shots at the extremely reasonable price of $175.

Notice the tremendous amount of information that has been packed into this multitude of single-word and phrase modifiers. There are enough ideas here to make two or three complete sentences. Rewrite the example. _____

Here's one way to do it:

> Wouldn't one of our golden retriever pups make an ideal Christmas gift for your son or daughter this year? These two-month-old animals came from Ardmor Kennels' registered champion stock, complete with papers and all shots. Your children can have one of these affectionate, loyal pets for the extremely reasonable price of $175.

Now begin the exercises.

EXERCISES

Use your mask here.

A   Many of the ideas in the following sentences have not been given proper impor-tance. Rewrite these sentences by giving each idea a form which reflects its relative importance. For instance, give lesser importance to the letter reference (now a main statement) in the example below.

1   I have your letter of August 11, which has many useful suggestions.

You are correct if you gave lesser importance to the letter reference by placing it in a clause or phrase. Or you are correct if you made "letter" the subject of your main statement.

> In *your letter of August 11*, you give (I found) many useful suggestions (in your letter of August 11).
>
> or
>
> *Your August 11 letter* gives (has) many useful suggestions.

2   These machines should not be allowed to run faster than their specified limits, and these limits are in the enclosed handbook.

You are correct if you gave lesser importance to the idea in the second main statement.

> These machines should not be allowed to run faster than the (specified) limits specified *in the enclosed handbook.*

3   Those who regularly use this product have established its reputation for durability.

You are correct if you converted the idea in the clause to "regular users."

Regular users of this product have established its reputation for durability.

4   I have a person who is an electrical engineer and who is on my staff.

You are correct if your sentence has no clauses in it.

I have *an electrical engineer on my staff.*

5   Our Men's Shop is offering a sale of tweed suits which starts today and which lasts two weeks.

You are correct if your sentence has no clauses in it.

Starting today, our Men's Shop is offering a *two-week* sale of tweed suits (starting today).

or

Today, our Men's Shop *starts* a *two-week* sale of tweed suits.

6   This offer is an unusual one, and it will not be repeated.

You are correct if you reduced the idea in the first main statement to some sort of modifier.

This *unusual* offer will not be repeated.

7   The committee, which is made of vice presidents and which is called the executive committee, has not discussed the problem.

You are correct if you reduced the two clauses to phrase or single-word modifiers.

The executive committee, made up of vice presidents, (of vice presidents) has not discussed the problem.

or

The *vice presidents of the executive committee* have not discussed the problem.

8   The deluxe model comes in red, blue, or black, and it sells for $5,000 more.

The cost of the product is much more important than its color. You should have . .

1   Given the colors less importance

2   Made the cost part of the first main statement.

> The deluxe model, in red, blue, or black, *sells* for $5,000 more.

9   This new oven is large, and it will hold your biggest Thanksgiving turkey.

You are correct if you gave lesser importance to "large" and combined the two main statements.

> This *large* new oven *will hold your biggest Thanksgiving turkey.*
>
> or
>
> This new oven is *large* enough to hold your biggest Thanksgiving turkey.

10   The following example is different from the others in this exercise in that it is oversubordinated rather than undersubordinated. That is, the large number of subordinate clauses and phrases make it too long. Break it into at least *two* sentences.

> The rule book, designed to help sales managers interpret company policy, will be displayed at their meeting on July 10, with Mr. White available to answer questions about it.

You should have written at least two complete sentences.

> The rule book is designed to help sales managers interpret company policy. It will be displayed at their meeting on July 10. (, and) Mr. White will be available (will answer) to answer questions about it.

HELPFUL HINT

Go over the modifiers in your next first-draft letter and test each idea to see if you have given it its proper importance. If you find some ineffectively expressed ideas, write them in a different form.

NINE
USE PARALLELISM CORRECTLY

I know of no more valuable asset in business life than the ability to express one's thoughts with clarity and precision.

John T. Connor, Chairman of the Board,
Allied Chemical Corporation

Use your mask here.

THE CONCEPT OF *PARALLELISM*

1   Few devices available to the letter writer are so helpful, so frequently applicable, so strengthening to his writing as parallelism. Consider this list:

   A. flower
   B. leaf
   C   stone
   D. branch

All these words, except one, have something in common. Which is the discordant item?_____

   C

2a   Now look at this list:

   A. to swim
   B. to bowl
   C. to skate
   D. skiing

Each of these ideas has the same grammatical form, except one. It is _____ .

   D

2b   Does the *idea* expressed by the above dissimilar form have something in common with the other three ideas? _____

   Yes (They all have something to do with sports.)

3   If ideas have something in common, they are said to be *parallel.*

   A. high
   B. low
   C. green

Which of these ideas are parallel? _____

   A and B

4   If one form in a sentence is identical to another form, these forms are *also* said to be parallel.

   A. in the house
   B. barn
   C. in the garage

Which of these forms are parallel?_____

   A and C (Both are phrases.)

TECHNIQUES OF PARALLELISM

5a   Here's the principle:

   Express parallel ideas in parallel forms.

Read the following sentence.

> Secretaries are expected to *receive callers*, to *answer telephones*, and *miscellaneous clerical work must be done.*

Are all three of the italicized ideas things that secretaries may be expected to do?

Yes

5b Are all three of these *ideas* parallel? _____

Yes

5c Notice the *form* of the last idea. Is it identical to the other two forms?

No

5d Parallel ideas should be expressed in parallel form. Change "miscellaneous clerical work must be done" so that it conforms with the two phrases. _____

> to do (perform) miscellaneous clerical work

6

> All inspectors were given training in handling investigations and how to interpret findings.

Since the inspectors were given training in two similar things, they should be expressed in parallel forms. Rewrite the sentence.

> The inspectors were given training *in handling* investigations and *in interpreting* findings.

or

> The inspectors were given training in *how to handle* investigations and in *how to interpret* findings.

REPEATING THE INTRODUCTORY WORD

7a Here is the last paragraph of a sales letter written by the president of the Electronics Components Corporation to a government agency. The letter accompanies a bid for a government contract.

> Electronics Components Corporation *offers* years of practical experience but remains at the frontier of electronics research, *offers* the highest production standards but always delivers before a deadline, *offers* the highest quality components but sells at lowest prices.

Notice the three identical verbs. Are the constructions that follow these verbs parallel? _____

Yes

7b What word signals three other parallel constructions? _____

---

but

7c   Does this parallelism help the writer to drive home the points in his letter?

_____

Yes (We think so.)

8   Don't hesitate to repeat the introductory word of each parallel form. It's a signal which tells your reader, "here are some related ideas that I've placed in parallel forms." Sometimes, of course, you may want to use the introductory word in only the first of a series of parallel forms.

We must teach everything about preparing for the interview, meeting the prospect, and following up the sale.

This is all right, but the similarity of the ideas would be emphasized if you signaled the parallelism with the same introductory word, as in:

We must teach everything *about* preparing for the interview, *about* meeting the prospect, and *about* following up the sale.

Here's another point: any sentence may contain the following parallel forms:

A.   parallel main statements
B.   parallel clauses
C.   parallel phrases
D.   parallel single words

Label each of the sentences below with the letter of the type of parallel form demonstrated.

1   He entered, his body shivering, his hands shaking, his teeth chattering. _____
2   We want a man who knows accounting and who will accept responsibility. _____
3   The storeroom boxes have fallen down, and the men are picking them up. _____
4   This man is strong, intelligent, and alert. _____

1   C
2   B
3   A
4   D

CORRECTING MISTAKES IN PARALLELISM

9a

After the director told the staff to gather more information, he told them they would have to organize it and write a report.

How many different things did the director tell the staff to do? _____

three

9b   Rewrite the above sentence by using "the director told the staff" as your main statement and by placing the three parallel ideas in a series of parallel forms.

_____

The director told the staff *to* gather more information, *to* organize it, and *to* write a report.

9c   Which sentence is more concise? The revision or the original?_____

the revision

10

The supervisor will study the report before the committee does, and finally the director himself will look at it.

This sentence has three parallel ideas which haven't been placed in parallel forms. Place these ideas in parallel forms. They do not have to be parallel main statements.

_____

You are correct if you placed the three "studiers" in parallel forms.

First the *supervisor*, then the *committee*, and finally the *director* himself will study the report.

or

The report will be studied *by the supervisor* first, then *by the committee*, and finally *by the director* himself.

11a   Look at the following sentence:

The effective writer always *plans* beforehand, *revises* carefully, and *does not forget* the reader.

Are the three forms in this sentence parallel?_____

Yes

11b   Which of the three ideas is negative?_____

the last, the third

11c   Generally, a series of parallel ideas will read a little more smoothly if they are all positive or negative. So add a refinement. Change "does not forget" to "_____" to make it positive.

remembers

12   In previous chapters you have seen that a being verb in a linking sentence can relate the subject with another idea. For instance:

The profits *are* large.

In the above case, the two ideas linked by "are" are not parallel. One is a noun, the other an adjective. But sometimes a being verb does link parallel forms. For instance:

To write is *to struggle* with ideas.

Both of the above ideas are parallel, and they are expressed in parallel forms. But notice the following example:

Learning to reel off a rule by heart is not necessarily *to master* it.

"Learning" and "to master" are parallel ideas, but they are not expressed in parallel forms. Rewrite the sentence by making the two forms parallel._____

Learning to reel off a rule by heart is not necessarily *mastering* it.

or

To learn to reel off a rule by heart is not necessarily *to master* it.

13 "Not only . . . but also" is often used to show a relationship between parallel ideas: *not only* such and such *but also* this and that. If we show this relationship, "such and such" must be parallel to "this and that."

We intended not only *to obtain* information relevant to the case but also *securing* background material was aimed at.

"Not only" and "but also" are followed by forms which are not parallel. Correct the situation. _____

We intended not only *to obtain* information relevant to the case but also *to secure* background material.

or

We not only *intended* to obtain information relevant to the case, but (also) we also *aimed* at securing background material.

14

It was *not only* Peabody's poor planning, *but also* he failed to make an estimate.

The forms following "not only" and "but also" are not parallel. Correct the sentence. _____

Peabody not only *planned* poorly but also *failed* to make an estimate.

or

Not only *did Peabody plan poorly* but also *he failed to make an estimate.*

or

It was not only Peabody's poor *planning* but also his *failure (failing)* to make an estimate.

15 "Rather than" is also useful for showing parallel relationships, as in:

Management has decided to *expand* the old plant rather than *buy* a new one.

Be sure that the ideas on each side of "rather than" have parallel form.

This office decided to help the research effort rather than acting as a drag on it.

Correct this sentence. _____

This office decided to *help* the research effort rather than (to) *act* as a drag on it.

THE LAST ITEM IN A PARALLEL SERIES

16 Generally, the longest of a series of parallel forms should come last.

The customer bought boots, $100 worth of fishing tackle, and hats.

Make this a little smoother. _____

The customer bought boots, hats, and $100 worth of fishing tackle.

17 Sometimes a short last form will lend ironic emphasis.

The salesmen were not paid, were not given essential training aids, and were not given thorough instruction.

Put the short, important item last. _____

The salesmen were not given essential training aids, were not given thorough instruction, and *were not paid*.

The following sentences are memorable partly because they use parallelism:

But, in a larger sense, we cannot dedicate, we cannot consecrate, we cannot hallow this ground.
Abraham Lincoln, *The Gettysburg Address*

For thine is the kingdom, and the power, and the glory, for ever.
The Lord's Prayer

As Caesar loved me, I weep for him;
As he was fortunate, I rejoice at it;
As he was valiant, I honour him;
But as he was ambitious, I slew him.
William Shakespeare, *Julius Caesar*, III. ii.

Now begin the exercises.

EXERCISES

Use your mask here.

A   Give the parallel ideas in the following ten sentences parallel form.

1 He gave instructions first to check the work thoroughly and then for revising it.

He gave instructions (to) first *to check* the work thoroughly and then (to) *revise* it.

or

He gave instructions first *for checking* the work and then *for revising* it.

2 This new product offers these advantages—easy operation, durability, and is economical.

You are correct if you . . .

1 Converted "is economical" to "economy"
2 Placed "easy operation," the longest item, last

This new product offers these advantages—*durability, economy,* and *easy operation.*

3 We made this offer with a twofold purpose—to stimulate dealer sales and for the education of the individual customer.

We made this offer with a twofold purpose—*to stimulate* dealer sales and *to educate* the individual customer.

4 He is a conscientious, hardworking employee who cooperates well.

He is a *conscientious, hardworking,* (and) *cooperative* employee.

5 To write correctly is not necessarily writing effectively.

To write correctly is not necessarily *to write* effectively.

or

Writing correctly is not necessarily *writing* effectively.

6 Once the apples have been pared and sliced, sprinkling with granulated sugar is advisable before you put them in the pie crust.

You are correct if the three steps have parallel forms.

The apples should be pared and sliced, (then) sprinkled with granulated sugar, and placed in the pie crust.

or

Pare and slice the apples; (then) sprinkle them with granulated sugar; and then put them in the pie crust.

7 All accounting personnel and those in shipping and sales will report to Room 101 at three o'clock.

You are correct if the three groups have parallel forms.

All accounting, sales, and shipping personnel will report to Room 101 at three o'clock.

or

All personnel in accounting, shipping, and sales will report to Room 101 at three o'clock.

8 The company not only has established an excellent reputation for research but also for pursuing an aggressive sales policy.

Notice that the following two answers do not have the same meaning. The original sentence, therefore, is ambiguous.

The company not only *has established* an excellent reputation for research but (also) *has pursued* an aggresssive sales policy.

and

The company has established an excellent reputation not only *for research* but (also) *for pursuing* an aggressive sales policy.

9 We landed a contract with them on June 18 after we learned of their training problem and analyzed it.

You are correct if you expressed the three actions in parallel forms.

We learned of their training problem, *analyzed* it, and (, on June 18,) *landed* a contract with them on June 18.

10   Mr. Maris wanted to pay cash immediately rather than delaying the transaction.

Mr. Maris wanted *to pay* cash immediately rather than *(to) delay* the transaction.

HELPFUL HINT

Go over your next first-draft letter and look at each idea in relation to the other ideas in the sentence. If any are parallel, make sure they have parallel forms.

TEN
USE THE RIGHT LINK
FOR CLARITY

Today's leaders are frequently men and women who
have mastered the art of communication. They know
how to get their ideas across. And successful
people—those who are continually sought for key
positions—effectively combine their ability to
communicate with a solid foundation of knowledge. For
knowledge is the predominant quality in the
transmission of ideas.

Robert W. Sarnoff, Chairman, RCA Corporation

Use your mask here.

THE MEANING OF LINKS

1a   Here is a list of links.

1   and
2   but
3   or
4   for
5   nor

These words, if used effectively, can make your writing easier to understand. To the reader, they are signals which tell him how one idea relates to another. Examine the following statements.

A.   We bid for the contract;
B.   we did not win it.

Notice A   It expresses a (positive/negative) idea. _____

---
a positive

1b   Notice B   It expresses a (positive/negative) idea. _____

---
a negative

1c   Now let's look at the relationship between the two ideas. Since A is positive and B is negative, B is (a contrasting/an additional) idea. _____

---
a contrasting

1d   We can now insert one of the above links between the two ideas to show the reader this contrasting relationship. Fill in the right link in the following sentence.

We bid for the contract, _____ we did not win it.

---
but

2a   Do both A and B below express positive ideas? _____

A.   We bid for the contract;
B.   we won it.

Yes

2b   B is (a contrasting/an additional) idea. _____

---
an additional

2c   We bid for the contract, (but/and) we won it. _____

---
and

3a   When you want to link two ideas and the second idea is simply an additional idea, you use "_____."

---
and

3b   When you want to link two ideas and the second idea is a contrasting idea, you use "_____."

---
but

4 Insert the appropriate link in the following:

The new conveyor belt saves time, _____ it is expensive to maintain.

---

but

5 Fill in the proper link in the following:

Mr. Luce is a top-notch salesman, _____ he is not very reliable.

---

but

6a Here's another type of linking situation:

A. We can give you a $50 refund
B. we can credit this $50 to your account.

Idea B is (a contrasting/an alternative) idea. _____

---

an alternative

6b

and
but
or
for
nor

What is the link which will signal that the second idea above is an alternative?

---

or

7a When the reader sees "and," he knows that the next thought will be merely a/an _____ thought.

---

an additional

7b When the reader sees "but," he knows that the next thought will be a/an _____ thought.

---

a contrasting

7c When the reader sees "or," he knows that the next thought will be a/an _____ thought.

---

an alternative

8

A. I recommend that we hold the bazaar indoors this year,
B. it may rain.

Above, idea B *supports* idea A. Choose the link below which will show this supporting relationship.

I recommend that we hold the bazaar indoors this year, (or/for/and/but) it may rain.

---

for

9 "Nor" is very handy for linking two negative ideas. Look at the following sentence:

The invoice was not discovered until Friday, *and* it was not mailed until the following Monday.

"And" is not too bad in this sentence, but "nor" will emphasize the two negative thoughts better. For example:

The invoice was not discovered until Friday, *nor* was it mailed until the following Monday.

Rewrite the following sentence, using "nor": _____

The breakdown of the power units did not halt work in the mines, and it did not decrease production.

The breakdown of the power units did not halt work in the mines, *nor* did it decrease production.

10   Match the link with the kind of relationship it announces to your reader.

Link	Relationship
1 And _____	A. Here is an alternative thought.
2 Or _____	B. Here is a contrasting thought.
3 But _____	C. Here is a supporting thought.
4 Nor _____	D. Here is another negative thought.
5 For _____	E. Here is an additional thought.

---

1   E

2   A

3   B

4   D

5   C

11   Choose the right link for each of the following:

A.   I folded the letter, _____ placed it in the envelope.

B.   I wrote him, _____ he did not write to me.

C.   You may write to him, _____ you may call him, but not both.

D.   It must be late, _____ I am hungry.

E.   It is not late, _____ is it early.

A.   and

B.   but

C.   or

D.   for (You are also right if you said "and.")

E.   nor

USE LINKS PRECISELY

12a   When you write, you may not think very much about showing your reader how your ideas relate to each other. Most likely, you automatically insert "and's" and "but's" because they seem to fit. However, linking is not always as simple as it seems. For the relationship between ideas may sometimes be neither necessary nor obvious. For instance, the following sentence shows a relationship that we have not yet discussed.

> Please tell us if our assumption is incorrect, *and* we will further adjust your contract.

At first glance this use of "and" seems to be all right. But notice that the two ideas on each side of "and" are not simply additive. Rather, the second idea (depends on/contrasts with) the first.

---

depends on

12b "And" should not be used when you can show a more specific relationship. So rewrite the above sentence by placing the first idea in a conditional "if" clause.

> If you tell us our assumption is incorrect, we will further adjust your contract.
>
> or
>
> If our assumption is incorrect, we will further adjust your contract.

13a Read this sentence carefully.

> The search for a new synthetic fiber has been difficult and expensive, *and* further investigation should produce great rewards.

In this sentence the idea following "and" is a/an _____ idea.

---

a contrasting (The first idea is negative, the second is positive.)

13b In this sentence, "and" should be replaced with "_____."

---

but

14 Generally, do not use two "but's" in the same sentence. The last idea is a contrast on a contrast. Revise the following sentence. _____

> We haven't accomplished very much, *but* I feel tired already, *but* I am willing to go on.

Any reasonable version is correct as long as you did not use two "but's."

> *Although* we haven't accomplished very much, I feel tired already; *but* I am willing to go on.
>
> or
>
> *Although* we haven't accomplished very much *and* I feel tired already, I am willing to go on.

LINKS AT THE BEGINNING OF A SENTENCE

15 You may have been told not to begin a sentence with links such as "and," "but," etc. *But* why not? Sometimes you may find that you've written a long sentence with two main statements that are linked by "and" or "but." Long sentences tire your reader. To give him a breather, you may want to do what professional writers often do: split the sentence and start a second sentence with a link.

The following sentence should be split. What word would start the second sentence? _____

We have a large task ahead of us which presents many challenging problems, but I believe we will overcome difficulties if we obtain the money.

but

MORE LINKS

16a   Here's another list of links:

1   furthermore
2   however
3   therefore
4   consequently
5   similarly

Like *and, but, or, for,* and *nor,* the above links are useful for showing specific relationships between ideas. Read the following:

A.   He has been on time every day for two weeks;
B.   he punched the time clock correctly.

Of course you could use "and" to signal the additional idea, but one of the above links can do just as well. Which one? _____

furthermore

16b   Use one of the new links in the following:

They tried to increase the interest rate; _____ , they didn't have the authority to do so.

however

17a   Read the following:

A.   All reports must be handed in by Tuesday, and Jones is one of those writing a report.
B.   Jones must hand in his report by Tuesday.

The idea expressed in B (follows logically from/is the result of) the ideas in A.

_____

follows logically from

17b

All reports must be handed in by Tuesday, and Jones is one of those writing a report. (Therefore/Consequently), Jones must hand in his report by Tuesday.

therefore

17c   "Therefore" usually tells the reader that an idea (follows logically from/is the result of) another. _____

follows logically from

18a Read this:

A. The worker was felled by a brick which dropped from the roof of the tower.

B. He spent six weeks in the hospital.

Idea B (follows logically from/is the result of) idea A.

---

is the result of

18b

The worker was felled by a brick which dropped from the roof of the tower. (Therefore/Consequently), he spent six weeks in the hospital.

---

consequently

18c "Consequently" usually signals that one idea is _____ another.

---

the result of

18d "Therefore" usually signals that one idea _____ another.

---

follows logically from

19

A sealed cellophane wrapper will keep lettuce fresh. _____, a sealed plastic envelope will preserve valuable documents indefinitely.

The second thought is similar to the first. What is the link that should be placed in the blank in the above sentence? _____

---

similarly, likewise

20a Read the following sentence carefully:

For several years, the rural families ate nothing but polished rice, *and* rickets was widespread.

Is the idea in the second main statement simply an additional idea? _____

No

20b Might rickets be the result of eating polished rice? _____

Yes

20c To make certain that the reader is aware of this cause and effect relationship, you should insert the link, "_____."

---

consequently

21 Read this:

The Devlon Company will merge with the Nertial Corporation on October 12. We have eight days to get the documents ready, therefore.

Unlike links such as *and* or *but*, links such as *therefore* or *consequently* can be placed in various positions within a sentence. Notice where "therefore" is placed in the second sentence. It's supposed to show that the idea in this sentence follows logically from the first. However, the reader doesn't discover this until the end.

There are several good places near the front of the second sentence where you can reposition "therefore." Rewrite it. _____

Therefore, we have eight days to get the documents ready.

or

We have, *therefore*, eight days to get the documents ready.

or

We *therefore* have eight days to get the documents ready.

22 Match the link with the kind of relationship it announces to your reader.

Link	*Relationship*
1 And, moreover, furthermore, also _____	A. Here comes a contrasting idea.
	B. Here comes an idea that is the result of a previous idea.
2 But, however, nevertheless _____	C. Here comes an idea that follows logically from the previous idea.
3 Consequently _____	
4 Therefore _____	D. Here comes an additional idea.
5 Likewise, similarly _____	E. Here comes a similar idea.
6 For _____	F. Here comes a supporting idea.
7 Or _____	G. Here comes an alternative idea.

---

1 D
2 A
3 B
4 C
5 E
6 F
7 G

23 "I don't get the connection. This is unclear; it's choppy." Have you ever said something like that to yourself as you were reading? If you have, most likely the writer did not use *enough* links to signal the relationships between his ideas.

Why? Because, as he proceeds with the relatively slow process of writing, a writer often becomes so familiar with the ideas he's trying to communicate that the relationships between them are obvious to him. Consequently, the *therefore's* and *but's* seem unnecessary. The reader's eye, however, travels swiftly along a sentence, and he needs these signals as much as the motorist needs road signs.

The following paragraph is underlinked. First read it all the way through.

Certainly, we had some encouraging economic developments in October. 1 _____ , we must be a little cautious before concluding that a new phase of rising business activity is underway. Industrial production did not increase in October nor did factory payrolls. 2 _____ , the length of the workweek declined. These negative indications must be balanced against the higher earnings reported by several of our giant corporations. I conclude, 3 _____ , that our economy will surge ahead cautiously.

Now insert the appropriate links and note how much more smoothly the paragraph reads.

1   However, But
2   Furthermore, Moreover, In addition, Also, Similarly
3   therefore

Now begin the exercises.

EXERCISES

Use your mask here.

A   Insert appropriate links in the following sentences .

1   She was late to work _____ was able to type the speech by twelve o'clock.

but

2   You can withdraw your dividends, _____ you can leave them with us to accumulate interest.

or

3   Pottersby Ltd. will soon have several top-level job openings, _____ their sales force is expanding.

for

4   Patrons are not permitted to borrow books, _____ may they take them from the reading room.

nor

5   A citywide advertising campaign will cost about $75,000 but will increase sales by about $300,000; _____ , we should undertake this campaign.

therefore

6   Hicks has worked long and hard on these plans; _____ , he has done an outstanding job. _____ , we must postpone the starting date of the project until next March.

and, furthermore, moreover
however, but, nevertheless

7   The pressure of work eased; _____ , we decided to devote some time to departmental problems.

consequently

8   The new clause concerning forfeits does not really give your client full protection. It does, _____ , make it somewhat more difficult for him to be damaged by irresponsible parties.

however, nevertheless

9   Our agreement reads that the deadline must be met or you must notify us of a delay at least ten days before the deadline. Your particular deadline is only two days away. _____ , you must meet the deadline_____ consider our agreement void.

Therefore, Hence, Thus
or

10   It was a very well-written report, _____ it took him almost two months to finish.

but

HELPFUL HINT

After you revise the first draft of your next letter, put it aside for at least a few hours. Then return to it and read it for smoothness. You may find that you have left out some important links.

SUMMARY EXERCISE FOR PART I

Below is an exercise that provides practice in using all the skills covered in Part I. It may take as long as half an hour.

The following letter has one or more samples of each writing fault we have covered so far. In it, you will find at least one example of

1   incorrect usage
2   unnecessary usage
3   wordy usage
4   archaic usage
5   inflated usage
6   vague or general usage
7   a weak sentence caused by a being verb
8   a weak sentence caused by a general action verb
9   a weak passive sentence
10   a wordy clause
11   a misplaced modifier
12   a dangling modifier
13   a lesser idea that has been given the wrong importance
14   parallel ideas placed in unparallel form
15   a linking error

First read the whole letter. Then, taking your time with each sentence, detect and identify to yourself the various faults. Then rewrite the letter sentence by sentence.

Simulator Typewriter Company
158 Megaton Avenue
Flint, Michigan 48505

June 14,

Mr. David Abraham
Manager
Claims Division
Tokay Railroad
Blattsville, Mississippi 38672

Dear Mr. Abraham:

1 On the date of January 25, shipment of a crate of seventy-five of our Zippo Electric Typewriters to Yescourt Life Insurance Co. in the city of Sacramento was made by Mr. Mays, who is your shipping agent.   **2** Six days subsequent to the above date, damage to a vast majority of the machines was sustained when one of your Chicago crane operators dropped the crate.

3 February 16 was the date that a Freight Damage Claim in the amount of $3,500 was sent by mail by me to Mrs. Marcella in your Claims Division.   **4** Writing me in return, I was advised that she would give my claim special attention and settlement no doubt being received by me at the earliest possible date.

5 A period of two months occurred, and on April 17, I affected an inquiry in re the claim to Mrs. Marcella.   **6** A form postcard came advising me, three weeks subsequent to my inquiry, that processing of my claim was underway and that my patience would be appreciated.   **7** That was one month in the past, and no further contact has been made or any remittance either.

8 I personally think that it ought to be brought to your attention that replacement had to be made to Yescourt.   **9** And the cost of repairing sixty-eight of the damaged typewriters was absorbed by us.   **10** Therefore 't was necessary to get rid of them at prices that were greatly reduced.

11 Very soon, I would like to have your reply, or what would be better would be a check for $3,500.

Sincerely yours,

---

1 On January 15, your shipping agent, Mr. Mays, shipped a crate of seventy-five of our Zippo Electric Typewriters to the Yescourt Life Insurance Company in Sacramento.

You are correct if you . . .

1 Omitted "the date of"
2 Used a specific action verb in place of "was made"
3 Made the sentence active
4 Omitted "the city of"
5 Reduced the wordy "who" clause to "shipping agent"

2 Six days later, one of your Chicago crane operators damaged almost every typewriter by dropping the crate.

You are correct if you . . .

1 Deflated "subsequent to the above date"
2 Used either "to damage" or "to drop" in place of the general action verb, "to sustain"
3 Deflated "a vast majority"

3 On February 16, I mailed a Freight Damage Claim for $3,500 to Mrs. Marcella in your Claims Division.

You are correct if you . . .

1 Converted the main statements to the modifying phrase, "on February 16"
2 Used "to mail" as the main verb
3 Wrote an active sentence
4 Replaced "in the amount of" with "for"

4 She wrote me that she would give my claim special attention and that I would no doubt receive settlement soon.

You are correct if you . .

1 Eliminated the dangling modifier
2 Deflated "advised"
3 Wrote an active sentence
4 Placed the two parallel ideas in parallel form
5 Replaced "earliest possible date" with "soon"

5 Two months passed, and on April 17, I sent an inquiry about the claim to Mrs. Marcella.

You are correct if you . . .

1 Omitted "a period of"
2 Used a more specific action verb in place of "occurred" or eliminated it
3 Used an action verb in place of the incorrect verb, "to affect"
4 Replaced the archaic "in re" with "about"

6 Three weeks later, I received a form postcard telling me that my claim was being processed and that my patience would be appreciated.

You are correct if you . . .

1 Deflated the misplaced modifier, "three weeks subsequent to my inquiry" and placed it at the front of the sentence
2 Replaced "advising" with "telling" or "informing"
3 Replaced "was underway" with "was being processed"

7 That was one month ago, and I still haven't heard a word nor received a check.

You are correct if you . . .

1 Shortened "in the past"
2 Deflated and made more specific "no further contact has been made"
3 Expressed the two ideas on each side of "or" in parallel form

> 8 I think you ought to know that I (we) had to replace the Yescourt typewriters.

You are correct if you . . .

1 Eliminated the doublet "personally think"
2 Deflated "brought to your attention" or eliminated it
3 Used "to replace" in place of the general action verb, "to make"
4 Made all subject-verbs active

> 9 And I (we) had to absorb the cost of repairing sixty-eight of the damaged typewriters.

You are correct if you wrote an active sentence.

> 10 Consequently, I (we) had to sell them at greatly reduced prices.

You are correct if you . . .

1 Used "consequently" instead of "therefore"
2 Replaced the being verb, "was," with a specific action verb
3 Wrote an active sentence
4 Reduced the wordy clause, "that were greatly reduced," to a phrase modifier

> 11 I would like to have your reply very soon, or better, receive your check for $3,500.

You are correct if you . . .

1 Placed "very soon" closer to the verb "have"
2 Simplified and shortened the second main statement

Your revised letter should read something like this:

Dear Mr. Abraham:

On January 25, your shipping agent, Mr. Mays, shipped a crate of seventy-five of our Zippo Electric Typewriters to the Yescourt Life Insurance Company in Sacramento. Six days later, one of your Chicago crane operators damaged almost every typewriter by dropping the crate.

On February 16, I mailed a Freight Damage Claim for $3,500 to Mrs. Marcella in your Claims Division. She wrote me that she would give my claim special attention and that I would no doubt receive settlement soon.

Two months passed, and on April 17, I sent an inquiry about the claim to Mrs. Marcella. Three weeks later, I received a form postcard telling me that my claim was being processed and that my patience would be appreciated.

That was one month ago, and I still haven't heard a word nor received a check.

I think you ought to know that I had to replace the Yescourt typewriters. And I had to absorb the cost of repairing sixty-eight of the damaged typewriters. Consequently, I had to sell them at greatly reduced prices.

I would like to have your reply very soon, or better, receive your check for $3,500.

Sincerely yours,

PART TWO
PLEASANT TONE

In Part 1 of this book we concentrated on teaching you ways to make your business letters easy to understand that is, clear, concise, and forceful. This part will show you how to achieve a pleasant tone, by being natural, courteous, friendly, and personal.

ELEVEN
BE NATURAL

The accurate transmission of ideas and facts from one mind to another is a complex process with many pitfalls, especially when the communication must be in writing. The man who wishes to advance in business must exert himself to improve his communications skill. His goal should be not merely to be understood but, if possible, to write so that he cannot be misunderstood.

Harry O. Bercher. President International Harvester Company

Use your mask here.

TONE

1   If you can write clearly, concisely, and forcefully, you have come a long way toward effective letter writing. Letters which have these qualities will not only be easily understood but will help you make a good impression on your reader. However, you cannot be sure that your letter will do this unless it has another ingredient: *pleasant tone*.

By "tone" we mean what your words *imply* as opposed to what they literally say. Tone is the sound of the writer's voice, and sometimes this sound may suggest something wholly different from the writer's literal meaning.

In conversation, tone plays an important role. For instance, suppose a merchant tells a customer when he will receive his merchandise. Walking out of the store, the customer might say to his friend: "He said I would have it by Tuesday, but from the way he said it (tone), I'll be lucky to have it a week from then."

In a letter, tone plays an equally important role. The following three letters all have the same literal meaning. But which has the most pleasant tone? _____

A.   I am sorry but it is not possible to send you any information concerning the procedure for using the Wide Eye Exposure Meter. We no longer distribute this item. All such inquiries are now handled by Mr. Custer, Flick Photo Distributors, 211 Pew Street, Chicago, Illinois. It would be appreciated if you would write to him in the future.

B.   I'm sorry that I'm not able to answer your questions about your Wide Eye Exposure Meter, since we no longer distribute this item. If you will write to Mr. Custer, Flick Photo Distributors, 211 Pew Street, Chicago, Illinois, he will be glad to give you the information you want.

C.   Oh boy, did you goof! You wrote the wrong place if it's info on the Wide Eye Exposure Meter that you want. We don't carry this item any more. Try Mr. Custer, Flick Photo Distributors, 211 Pew Street, Chicago, Illinois. He'll set you straight.

B (Letter A does not have a pleasant tone because it is too abrupt and formal. The last sentence is particularly bad because it implies that the reader is being a nuisance. Letter C, on the other hand, is much too flip and breezy—many readers would be offended. Letter B has an appropriate tone for a business letter—not too familiar nor too stiff. It's pleasant.)

BUSINESS JARGON

2   Among the qualities that contribute to a pleasant tone is *naturalness*. Natural writing doesn't call attention to itself; it has the easy simplicity of conversation.

One of the greatest enemies of natural writing is business jargon. This artificial, stuffy style was acceptable fifty years ago when business was conducted on a more formal basis. Yet jargon is still with us today. Give the jargoneer something easy to say and this is how he says it:

In re your letter of November 21, in connection with our account, we are remitting our check herewith as per your request in the amount of $110.15. Find out what this jargoneer is trying to say with his business jargon and translate it into English. _____

> As you asked in your letter of November 21, we are enclosing our check for $110.15.

3 So far, you have seen a one-sided picture of the principles and techniques of effective letter writing. But now, in the interest of impartiality, the opposition will be given equal time. The following list of principles was taken from the *Jargoneer's Handbook*, a guide for apprentices who want to write with a "grand" style.

The Jargoneer's Checklist

1 Since original thoughts are hard to think of, use a cliché whenever possible.
2 Always substitute an archaic, pompous word for a contemporary, conversational word.
3 Use the general word instead of the specific. This keeps the reader awake, guessing at your meaning.
4 If you can think of a long, complicated word to take the place of a short, simple word, use the inflated word.
5 Make all active sentences passive.
6 Choose one type of sentence construction and never vary from it. This gives your letters a dull, monotonous tone—which has a certain dignity.

Some of the most natural, charming people in business become cold, pompous jargoneers when faced with the task of putting their words on paper. Why? Because they believe that a business letter will not be dignified or impressive unless they apply all the principles from the *Jargoneer's Handbook*. They inhibit their natural expressions and try to fit themselves into the mold that is called the "business writing style."

Actually, your style cannot be separated from what you say. It is not simply an added sauce for your dish of ideas. Your style should be *you*, an expression of your thought and personality. For a natural letter, like a natural person, is truly impressive.

The formula, then, for a natural style is to write the way you talk. Well, . . . almost. Here are three versions of the same sentence. Which version has the conversational, natural style appropriate to business letters? _____

A. We are in receipt of a letter from Mr. Tomas in connection with our action in issuing this contract with a rider.
B. Hello. This is Charley Freemont in A & S. Yes home office. What I'm calling about is the Tomas contract. Sorry, I'll spell it, T-O-M-A-S. Ok, I'll wait till you get it—hmm—well, he wrote us. He wants us to explain that rider on his contract.
C. We received a letter from Mr. Tomas today asking us to explain the rider in his contract.

> C (Sentence A is full of business jargon. Notice the hackneyed phrases such as "in receipt of" and "in connection with." Sentence B is like actual conversation. Real talk makes poor reading. Sentence C is easy to read because it maintains the simplicity of conversational language.)

WE DON'T DO IT THIS WAY ANY MORE

Order to Purchase and Ship Goods.

Boston, Oct. 2d, 18___.

Gentlemen — Will you please purchase for our account twenty-five 1/2 pipes Otard D. & Co. brandy, vintage 1870 (20 pale, 5 dark), at the prices stated in yours of the 27th ult.

In case you cannot obtain the dark brandy except in 1/4 casks, you may change the above order to 20 1/2 pipes pale and 10 1/4 casks dark, all of which you will please mark N.B. & Co., and forward by first clipper to Messrs. Newell Bros. & Co., San Francisco, Cal., immediately, giving us timely notice of shipment that we may effect insurance. You will oblige us greatly by endeavoring to have the packages as fresh-looking as possible, and putting the same in good order previous to sending them aboard the vessel. We desire that this consignment shall reach its destination in good condition. I particularly call your atten tion to this matter. Will remit sight draft upon receipt of invoice and bills of lading payable to order of Bank of America, in your city.

Respectfully yours,
C. Farley & Co.

—*Payne's Business Letter Writer and*
Book of Commercial Forms, 1884

WRITE THE WAY YOU TALK?

3a When we say, "write the way you talk," we mean that you should try to preserve, within the limitations of written communication, some of the freshness and warmth of the expressions you use in your conversations with others Look at the following:

> Dear Mr. Burton:
>
> With reference to yours of recent date would state that I am enclosing herewith our latest sales catalog. Should the need arise for any of our parts, we will feel gratified to fill an order for same.

Have you ever heard anyone talk like that? _____

> We hope not.

3b Rewrite it in conversational language. _____

You are correct if you . . .

1 Deflated "with reference to yours of recent date"
2 Omitted "would state"
3 Omitted "herewith"
4 Used the action verb, "to need," in place of the general action verb "to arise"
5 Deflated "we will feel gratified to fill your order for same"

> As you asked, I am enclosing our latest sales catalog If you need any parts, we will be happy to fill your order.

VISUALIZE YOUR READER

4a Another way you can achieve a natural style is to *visualize your reader*. A letter is your share of a conversation So imagine your reader is sitting across your desk from you and talk to him.

You can often find several clues to help you visualize your reader. For instance, if you're replying to his letter, it can tell you his name and where he lives; where he works, his occupation, his title (if his letter is on business stationery); something about his attitude (friendly, angry, nervous, pompous. etc.).

Or if your organization keeps a file on him, you can probably learn more specific details such as his age, his education, his marital status, number of children, etc. Most important, you might learn about his relationship with your firm. Is he an important customer? Is he a troublemaker? Has he been satisfied in the past?

Forgetting the reader is the main cause of letters that read as if they were produced by a machine. The writer forgets that his reader is, like himself, a human being. But with a little imagination, you can form a vivid image of your reader.

Let's apply our imagination to the following letter from a policy owner to an insurance company.

Lawton, Iowa
April 29,

Gentlemen.

Five days ago, I took my account book from the top drawer of my writing desk, where it has been kept all these years, and intended to mail it to you. But it is lost. I can't find it.

The only solution that I can think of is that it got mixed up in a pile of letters I was going through, and which I put in the kitchen range to burn. I've been so distressed about it, I couldn't sleep. It is not like I had lost it outside my home where someone could find it. But even the Lord can't restore a book that has been burned up. I suppose He could, but I don't think it will happen in my case.

I was eighty-four years old last Feb. 19. I have a good constitution, and I expect to live several years yet.

Will you make me a new book? And put in front of it that in case of my death, the insurance is to go to my husband. I have not told him that I lost the book. No need of both of us worrying.

Sincerely,
Nora Louise Calvin

This letter tells you a great deal about Mrs. Calvin. If you were going to reply to her letter, would you start with "We are in receipt of your communication dated April 29"? _____

No (We certainly hope not.)

4b Take a moment and think about Mrs. Calvin. What can you deduce about her from her letter? In about thirty words, give the essential facts about Mrs. Calvin and describe what kind of person she is. _____

Mrs. Calvin is an elderly lady from a rural town in Iowa. She is the wife of a farmer, probably. Although she is not highly educated, she is simple and honest. (Your reply should be natural, sympathetic, simple, and honest.)

LEVELS OF VOCABULARY

5 Writers also forget that what is easy and natural for one reader may be difficult for another. So watch the *level of vocabulary* in your letters. (We are not now talking about archaic, vague, or inflated words, which should always be eliminated.) We are talking about words which express your meaning perfectly, but which may confuse your reader because he does not have them in his vocabulary. An economics professor and a manual laborer may ask the same question about their taxes, but when you answer them, the level of vocabulary in each reply should be different.

Many letter writers are expert in a special field: insurance underwriting, space technology, internal revenue, to name a few. Each field has its own set of technical words. For this reason, insurance underwriters talk about "nonforfeiture options"; missile scientists about "gyro tumbling"; and tax experts about "store-keeper gaugers."

If you are a specialist and you are writing to a colleague, he will appreciate your technical terms. On the other hand, the ordinary reader doesn't like to read them, and for good reason. He doesn't understand them. Consequently, the specialist must be particularly careful to remember that his technical words, which are so familiar and valuable to him, may not be meaningful to the reader.

This does not mean that you should never use technical terms. But if you do and if you think your reader won't understand, then *explain* or *define* them. However, don't go to the opposite extreme of writing down to the reader by explaining in patronizingly childish terms.

Below are three versions of a letter from a major company to its stockholders. Which one has the proper level of vocabulary and the right amount of explaining?

Dear Stockholder:

A. In addition to the cash dividend, the Board of Directors of Maple Corporation has decided to award common stockholders a stock dividend. One hundred and fifty thousand shares will be distributed pro rata. Since you own three hundred shares, you will receive three additional shares as your stock dividend.

B. Each year we award cash dividends. Cash dividends are sums of money which the Board of Directors of Maple Corporation awards to every common stockholder. In addition to the cash dividend, the Board of Directors has decided to award a stock dividend. A stock dividend is like a cash dividend except payment is in shares of common stock instead of money.

   One hundred and fifty thousand shares will be distributed pro rata. This means that each stockholder will receive one additional share for each one hundred shares that he owns. Since you own three hundred shares, you will receive three additional shares as your stock dividend.

C. In addition to the cash dividend, the Board of Directors of Maple Corporation has decided to award common stockholders a stock dividend. One hundred and fifty thousand shares will be distributed pro rata. This means that each stockholder will receive one additional share for each one hundred shares that he owns. Since you own three hundred shares, you will receive three additional shares as your stock dividend.

C (Paragraph A may confuse some of the stockholders because it does not explain the term "pro rata." On the other hand, presentation B does too much explaining—since most stockholders already understand such items as "cash dividend" and "stock dividend." Paragraph C does explain the one term that needs an explanation—"pro rata."

SLANG AND COLLOQUIALISMS

6

> A lot of people who don't say "ain't," ain't eatin'.
>
> Will Rogers

Although many business writers err in the direction of a stiff formal style and would do well to follow the spirit of Mr. Rogers' comment. you should not, in your attempts to escape the jargoneer's formality, go overboard with indiscriminate use of slang or colloquialisms On the other hand, these expressions. when used prudently, will enliven the language of your business letters

Read the following two paragraphs and choose the one in which colloquialisms are tastefully used _____

A. Well, pal, here I am again with the lowdown about your disorderly cohorts at the sales convention in N'Yawk. We had a ball. And leading the pack was old Professor Andre who was stewed to the gills Somehow, he managed to give a bang-up speech on sales tactics

B   You'll be interested to know that Professor Andre's speech highlighted the sales convention in New York. He spoke about sales tactics and plans to do the same in a series of lectures in England this winter.

B (In paragraph A, the writer has tried unsuccessfully to affect a breezy manner by using too many slang expressions Paragraph B is appropriate to business writing.)

7a   Remember, you need not avoid *all* colloquialisms such as "catch on" for "understand" nor even slang expressions such as 'OK" for "all right." But you should be careful to use them sparingly.

The following paragraph has too many slang or colloquial expressions List all of them. _____

The workers in Section E have been sounding off about the increased work load. There's even been some talk about putting the screws on management to come up with a two-buck-an-hour hike in overtime pay.

sounding off (slang)
been some talk (colloquial)
come up with (colloquial)
putting the screws on (slang)
buck (slang)
hike (slang)

7b   Now write a substitute next to those expressions which you feel should be replaced. You do not have to replace all of them. _____

sounding off—complaining
been some talk
putting the screws on—asking, putting pressure on
come up with

buck—dollar

hike—raise, increase

(With the above changes, the paragraph should read as follows: "The workers in Section E have been complaining of the increased work load. There's even been some talk about asking management to come up with a two-dollar-an-hour raise in overtime pay.")

8   When you do use a colloquialism, do not call attention to it by enclosing it in quotes. To do so is to put on airs, to invite your reader to join a select group of people who know better.

The effective letter writer talks to his reader "man to man."

Rewrite this _____

The effective letter writer talks to his reader man to man.

CLICHÉS

9   A cliché is an expression which was once fresh and apt but which, through overuse and misuse, has become timeworn and hackneyed—lacking power to impress any but the most naïve reader. For instance:

crushing defeat	to withstand the test of time
cover a multitude of sins	swim like a fish
troubled times	conspicuous by its absence

We don't say that you should avoid clichés at all times. Sometimes a cliché will express your meaning quite adequately, as in, "He had to *thread his way* through a maze of machinery to find the broken lathe." However, when you use clichés repeatedly in a single letter, your reader may decide you lack originality or, even worse, are unable to think in other than stereotyped terms. Look at the following paragraph. How many clichés are in it?

I think we should explore every possible avenue of approach to the production problem at our East Hanover plant and should touch all bases with top management before we implement a decision. Your plan for retooling may be worth its weight in gold, but if installation costs get too high, we may be opening a can of worms. Nevertheless if you can demonstrate to my satisfaction that your plan will work, I'll back it up 120 percent to the powers that be.

eight (Here are the clichés in the above paragraph:

1   explore every possible avenue of approach

2   touch all bases

3   implement a decision

4   worth its weight in gold

5   opening a can of worms

6   demonstrate to my satisfaction

7   120 percent

8   the powers that be

If most of these clichés were eliminated, the letter would read something like this:

I think we should study all alternative solutions to the production problem at our East Hanover plant and should get top management's approval before we take action. Your plan for retooling may be the answer, but if installation costs get too high, we may only aggravate the problem. Nevertheless, if you can demonstrate to my satisfaction that your plan will work, I'll give it my full support to management.)

THE NATURAL WRITING PROCESS

Perhaps, after learning how to make your writing style more *natural*, you still have a doubt in the back of your mind. You have completed many chapters which helped you to discipline your writing. Now you may ask, "How can I be spontaneous and disciplined at the same time?"

The answer lies in the *natural writing process*. First write your idea into any sentence which seems to fit. At this stage spontaneity should reign. The natural writing process demands it.

The disciplining of the sentence—the testing and polishing of structure and language—all occur when you *revise* your letter.

> When one finds a natural style, one is amazed and delighted, for where one expected to see an author, one discovers a man.
>
> Blaise Pascal

Now begin the exercises.

EXERCISES

Use your mask here.

A Rewrite the following sentences to make them more natural.

1 If you will remit to us your canceled check or money-order stub, we will be in a position to determine how the aforementioned remittance was applied.

You are correct if you . . .

1 Used "send" for "remit"
2 Deflated "be in a position to determine"
3 Omitted "aforementioned"
4 Deflated "remittance"

> If you will send us your canceled check or money-order stub, we will be able to find out how we applied your payment.

2 So that settlement can be made without delay, please furnish the Mungiu letters in advance of December 14.

You are correct if you . . .

1 Made "settlement can be made" active
2 Deflated "without delay"
3 Deflated "furnish"
4 Substituted "before" for "in advance of"

> So that we (I) can make the settlement immediately, may we (I) have (please send us) the Mungiu letters before December 14?

3 I think we should meet on June 10 for a noodling session with Henry Middlebrook, who has conceptualized a viable rationale for building believability bridges between labor and management.

You are correct if you . . .

1 Replaced "noodling session"
2 Deflated "conceptualized a viable rationale"
3 Deflated "believability bridges"

> I think we should meet on June 10 with Henry Middlebrook, who has several good ideas on how to improve relations between labor and management.

4 Our own Mrs. Paulson from Public Relations has been busier than a mustard paddle at a weiner roast, working her fingers to the bone on a marketing survey in depth, which may show that our current ideas of customer buying habits are all wet.

You are correct if you . . .

1 Omitted "our own"
2 Toned down "busier than a mustard paddle at a weiner roast"
3 Eliminated the cliché, "working her fingers to the bone"
4 Replaced the slang expression "all wet" with something more appropriate

> Mrs. Paulson from Public Relations has been very busy with an exhaustive survey, which may show that our current ideas of customer buying habits are all wrong (erroneous, outmoded).

5 Referring to your communication of recent date, we wish to take this opportunity to state that the file folders about which you inquired were shipped as per your instructions on January 9.

You are correct if you . . .

1 Omitted "referring to your communication of recent date" or reduced it to the single-word modifier "recently"
2 Omitted "we wish to take this opportunity to state"
3 Deflated "inquired"
4 Omitted "as per your instructions"

The file folders which you recently asked about were shipped on January 9.

or

According to your instructions, we shipped the file folders on January 9.

6 In the event that this does not meet with your approval, please notify this writer as to your wishes.

You are correct if you . . .

1 Replaced "in the event that" with "if"
2 Deflated "does not meet with your approval"
3 Deflated "notify"
4 Replaced "this writer" with "me" or "I"
5 Deflated "as to your wishes"

If this is not right, let me know what you want to do.

or

Please let me know if you approve.

7 We have been endeavoring to ascertain the answer to the question as to whether or not Mr. Allen will pay us a visit in May.

You are correct if you . . .

1 Deflated "endeavoring to ascertain the answer to the question as to whether or not"
2 Reduced "pay us a visit" to "visit"

We've been trying to find out if Mr. Allen will visit us in May.

8 Due to the above-stated reasons, effectuation of a decision will have to be delayed by me until next month.

You are correct if you . . .

1 Deflated "due to the above-stated reasons"
2 Deflated "effectuation of a decision"
3 Wrote an active sentence

For these reasons (Therefore, Consequently), I must delay (making) my decision (hold off my decision) until next month.

9 The senior members of the medical team will say "so long" to their coworkers on Tuesday and will begin the first "leg" of their inspection tour, first stopping off in Mexico City.

You are correct if you at least removed the quotation marks.

The senior members of the medical team will say goodbye to their coworkers on Tuesday and will begin the first leg of their inspection tour, first stopping off in Mexico City.

10 This is just off the top of my head, but as I get it, we have three months to get this project off the ground before old man Parker gives it to us axewise.

You are correct if you . . .

1 Reduced "this is just off the top of my head, but as I get it" to "I think" or "I believe"
2 Changed "old man Parker" to "Mr. Parker"
3 Used another action verb in place of "gives it to us axewise"

> I think we have three months to get this project off the ground before Mr. Parker fires us

B Rewrite the following letter so that it is more natural

> Dear Mr. Huff:
>
> **1** Concerning the matter of your check for $19.02 which you mentioned in your letter of June 2, I referred this matter to our accounting department. **2** They have informed me that they are in possession of this canceled check which was endorsed as drawn with your signature.
>
> **3** It is possible that upon receipt of this letter, you may recall cashing this above-mentioned check. **4** If it is your belief, beyond a reasonable doubt, that this is not the case, there is the alternate possibility that an unknown individual intercepted your check and endorsed it with your signature.
>
> **5** If it is your desire, I can initiate an investigation into this contingency.
>
> Sincerely,

> **1** We have checked with our accounting department about the check for $19.02 which you mention in your letter of June 2.

You should have . . .

1 Deflated "concerning the matter of"
2 Deflated "referring this matter"

> **2** They tell us that they have the canceled check, endorsed with your signature.

You should have . . .

1 Deflated "informed"
2 Deflated and shortened "are in possession of"
3 Omitted "as drawn"

> **3** Could it be possible that you cashed the check and that this slipped your mind?

You should have . . .

1 Omitted "upon receipt of this letter"
2 Deflated "recall"
3 Omitted "above-mentioned"

4 If you are certain this is not so, someone may have intercepted your check and endorsed it.

You should have . . .

1 Deflated "if it is your belief"
2 Omitted "beyond a reasonable doubt"
3 Deflated "not the case"
4 Used "to intercept" as your main verb
5 Written an active sentence

5 If you wish, we can look into this possibility.

You should have . . .

1 Deflated "it is your desire"
2 Deflated "initiate an investigation"
3 Deflated "contingency"

HELPFUL HINT

After you have polished your next letter, read it aloud. After saying each sentence, ask yourself, "Is that the way I would say it if I were talking to him?" If it doesn't seem conversational, make it more natural.

"Now just couch that in legal phraseology and make three copies."

Reprinted from *The Wall Street Journal*.

TWELVE
BE COURTEOUS AND FRIENDLY

There is little risk of over-simplification in saying that good managers are good communicators; poor managers are usually the opposite. If an individual has a sincere desire to clarify his thinking, there is no better way to do it than to put it in writing.

Lawrence A. Appley, Chairman of the Board,
American Management Association

Use your mask here.

1 To many readers, a company seems too large and powerful. Because of this big-small relationship, readers are particularly offended by any bad manners or unfriendliness on the company's part. Conversely, they are almost always favorably impressed when they receive a business letter that is natural, friendly, and courteous.

Put yourself in the reader's place for a moment: you're leaving your home for work one morning. You stop at your mailbox and find a letter from Scardon's Department Store.

Which of the following would you rather read?

A. The store received your credit application form on time, but it was filled out incorrectly. As the form indicates, your signature should be written on the bottom of both pages, but you neglected to do this. Your form is being returned to you for further signature.

B. Thank you for returning your credit application form so quickly. However, we do need your signature on both pages. Just sign the second page at the bottom and return it. We'll be glad to consider your application.

B (Most readers do not like the kind of treatment they would receive in letter A. Notice the negative expressions such as "was filled out incorrectly" and "you neglected to do this." Sure, you made a mistake, but that's no reason for the harsh tone. Letter B, however, does not emphasize what you omitted to do but courteously points out what you can do to get an early decision on your credit application.)

COURTEOUS, FRIENDLY EXPRESSIONS

2 Courtesy in a business letter is important. And one obvious way to be courteous to your reader is to use courteous words. For instance, when your reader has said or done something for which you are grateful, simply say "_____."

thank you

3 To courteously ask your reader to do something for you, say "_____."

please

4 Although the opportunities to use "please" and "thank you" are numerous, these expressions never become trite or meaningless.

The following is a list of phrases often found in business letters. Some are desirable; others should be avoided. Choose the courteous or friendly phrases.

A. We are pleased . . .
B. I appreciate . . .
C. It is obvious that . . .
D. We suspect that . . .
E. You claim that . . .

F. Thank you for . . .
G. Please let me know if . . .
H. Will you please . . .
I. It should be clearly understood that . . .

J. May I ask you to . . . ?	O. We must . . .
K. It was nice of you to . . .	P. We are forced . . .
L. I am glad to . . .	Q. You forgot to . . .
M. I am sorry that . . .	R. You must realize that . . .
N. We are obliged to . . .	

A	J
B	K
F	L
G	M
H	

5   Read this sentence:

We need the construction estimates by the end of next week.

Here is a missed opportunity for the writer to do a little public relations work for his company. Rewrite this with a more courteous and friendly tone. _____

Please send us the construction estimates by the end of next week.

or

Could you send us the construction estimates by the end of next week?

6

Dear Mr. Veblin:

Bill Bunch told me that you visited him at his office and that you cleared up the dealer-price difficulty.

Obviously, Mr. Veblin has done the writer a favor. Rewrite this to include the courtesy that is missing in the opening sentence. _____

Thank you for clearing up the dealer-price difficulty.

or

I appreciate the visit you made to Bill Bunch to clear up the dealer-price difficulty. Thank you.

7   Sometimes, even the simple courtesies can go amiss. For if you use a word of courtesy inappropriately, the reader will think you're insincere.

In which of the following situations would it be inappropriate to thank a reader for his letter?

A.   The reader has written you saying how much he enjoys the new car you sold him.

B.   The outraged reader has written you saying that the new car you sold him is a lemon.

B (It's not appropriate to thank someone for a complaint.)

POSITIVE, NEGATIVE, AND NEUTRAL WORDS

8   One not-so-obvious way to be friendly and courteous is to use words with pleasant *overtones*. Words have two kinds of meaning. They have a dictionary

meaning, and they may also have overtones. For instance, the dictionary meaning of "to evict" is as follows:

> To put out a person or to recover by legal process, or by virtue of paramount right or claim; to eject.

But this word probably means much more than that to you. Many people, when they read the word "evict," may think of a widow with her six children sitting miserably in the rain on the sidewalk. "Evict" can give the reader these unpleasant associations because it has unpleasant overtones.

Because of the overtones a word may have, a word can be *positive* (pleasant) or *negative* (unpleasant). In addition, some words do not have any overtones at all and therefore are *neutral*.

Label the following words according to the kind of overtones they have for most people: positive, negative, or neutral.

1 Arrogant _____
2 Tactful _____
3 Large _____

---

1 negative
2 positive
3 neutral

9 Many words have few, if any, overtones for the reader. The word "another" probably means just that and nothing more to you. It is primarily a _____ word.

---

neutral

10 Words like "afraid," "unsuccessful," "delay," and "unhealthy" have unpleasant overtones. The reader's emotional reaction to these words can range from mild distaste to revulsion. They are _____ words.

---

negative

11 Words like "fair," "calm," "success," and "useful" usually have pleasant overtones. They are _____ words.

---

positive

12 Below, put a plus mark beside the positive words (most people like them), a minus sign beside the negative words (most people dislike them), and a zero beside the neutral words.

A. ability _____	J. genuine _____
B. worry _____	K. thanks _____
C. please _____	L. prohibit _____
D. unfair _____	M. indicate _____
E. regret _____	N. reject _____
F. punctual _____	O. harmony _____
G. book _____	P. pen _____
H. neglect _____	Q. loyalty _____
I. allege _____	R. hope _____

A.	+		J.	+
B.	−		K.	+
C.	+		L.	−
D.	−		M.	0
E.	−		N.	−
F.	+		O.	+
G.	0		P.	0
H.	−		Q.	+
I.	−		R.	+

Undertakers have taken to calling themselves "morticians," and butchers in some parts of the country prefer to be known as "meat cutters." Whenever one may think of the substitutions, they at least testify to the strength of connotations and the desire of men to avoid words with unpleasant or disparaging associations.

Brooks and Warren

13a   Now let's see what we can do about sentences containing negative words.

Dear. Mr. Portman:

We have found out that you are delinquent with regard to your account by $3.00.

Notice how unpleasant and unfriendly this opening is. "Found out" has the unpleasant overtone of "we've tracked you down, Mr. Portman."

The really insulting word, of course, is "_____."

delinquent

13b   Rewrite the above sentence so that the effect on the reader is at least neutral.

I notice that your account is short by $3.00. (There are no negative words in this sentence. "Short," by itself, is neutral.)

or

Your account shows a small deficit of $3.00. (Although "deficit" is somewhat negative, "small" shows your reader that you realize the amount is not terribly important, but the fact of your letter indicates the necessity of collection.)

14

In your letter of June 2, you claim that there were three witnesses to the accident. We need their names and addresses.

Notice how "claim" gives an unpleasant tone to the entire statement. "Claim" implies that the reader may have been lying about the witnesses, and that's the reason we need their names and addresses.

Rewrite these sentences, using only positive and neutral words._____

You are correct if you . . .

1   Used another word instead of "claim"

2   Made the request for action courteous

In your letter of June 2, you *mentioned (said, stated)* that there were three witnesses to the accident. May we have their names and addresses?

15

You are hereby requested to send payment of your gas bill by October 6.

"Yes, sir! Very good, sir! Nuts to you, sir!" is very likely to be the reader's reaction to this. Eliminate the offensive overtones. _____

Please send payment of your gas bill by October 6. (courteous)

or

May we have your payment of your gas bill by October 6? (courteous and friendly)

16

Since the deadline is February 15, a prompt reply before that date will be necessary.

Besides being in the passive voice, this is designed to antagonize. Use this opportunity to make a courteous request. _____

Since the deadline is February 15, may we hear from you before (by) then?

17a

We would have answered you sooner, but your letter was addressed to the wrong office.

What's the negative word here? _____

---

wrong

17b   "Wrong" implies that the reader was at fault. He may have been at fault, but why rub it in? Rewrite the sentence so that it is courteous and friendly. _____

We would have answered you sooner, but we just now received your letter from another office.

or

We would have answered you sooner, but your letter just now arrived from our other office.

ACCENT THE POSITIVE

18   The following sentence is not terribly unfriendly or discourteous, but "closed" is a negative word. Why not say the same thing by accenting the positive. Rewrite it. _____

Our office is closed after four o'clock.

Our office is *open* until four o'clock.

19   Words like "no," "not," and "cannot" are negative. Many times these words conceal a positive thought. You can often get rid of them by turning the thought around to make it positive.

We *cannot* have these figures for you before next week.

Why stress what we cannot do? Turn the thought around. _____

> We *will (can)* have these figures for you next week.

20   Sometimes you can't turn a negative thought completely around to make it entirely positive. For instance, consider this sentence:

> As you should know, we make no refunds after the three-month guarantee has run out.

The statement of this negative thought is unnecessarily arrogant and condescending. Soften the sentence. _____

> I'm sorry we cannot give you a refund because your three-month guarantee has run out. (This is still a little negative.)
> > or better
>
> I would like to give you a refund, but your three-month guarantee has run out.
> > or better yet
>
> We can only make refunds during the three-month guarantee period.

21

> We are forced to tell you that we cannot permit you to have another mortgage on your house.

Granted, this is a negative thought, but notice how harshly it is worded. See if you can soften the tone. _____

You are not wrong if you said "we wish to tell you that . . ." or "We would like to tell you that . . . ," but it is better to omit such expressions.

> I am sorry that we cannot give you another mortgage on your home.
> > or
>
> We feel that it's best for you to maintain only one mortgage on your home right now.

22a   Most of the ideas that a business writer communicates to his reader are factual. However, you should remember that even the most ordinary letter carries an element of emotion. This combination of emotion and objective fact will determine your reader's final impression (good or bad) of you and your organization.

Be especially careful when you have to deal explicitly with emotions or when you have to relate facts which have an emotional impact. There are many more of such situations than you might think. For example, a writer might have to tell a recent widow about the proceeds of her husband's life insurance policy. Or he may have to inform a supervisor that his best salesman has violated certain personnel practices.

So, particularly in emotional situations, take pains to use positive and neutral words and to avoid words with negative overtones.

The following is a letter from a subcontractor to a manufacturer of missiles:

Dear Mr. Germonn:

This is to inform you that the three rate-integrating gyros will not be ready by July 10 nor will we be able to deliver them until at least July 15. Since you specified such small tolerances, the precision machine work is taking longer than estimated.

This letter will undoubtedly inspire the reader with all the kindly instincts of a chicken hawk. Look at the first sentence. It tells the reader that they *cannot* do two things. Why be so negative? Revise the first sentence. _____

You are correct if you eliminated at least one of the negatives and if you softened the tone.

I am sorry but it will be at least July 15 before we can deliver the three rate-integrating gyros to you.

22b Notice the second sentence. This is even worse than the first because it tries to shift the blame for the delay to the manufacturer. Small tolerances may well be the cause of the delay, but the sentence should not imply that the manufacturer had no right to order such tolerances. Rewrite the sentence. _____

Because of the unusually small tolerances, the precision machine work is taking longer than we estimated.

23 By being aware of the overtones of the words you use, you can often soften the blow of a negative thought. Compare the following:

A. It is impossible for the Town of Ridgefield to permit your firm to construct its chemical plant on Wexler Road, because the stench will stifle those living nearby.

B. Because the fumes from your proposed chemical plant would disturb the people living near Wexler Road, we suggest that you consider building at one of our excellent industrial parks near Storm Watch Hill.

Which of these has the softer, more positive, tone? _____

B

24 Now list some of the negative words in the harsher version. _____

impossible, permit, stench, stifle, etc.

25 An unpleasant idea needs positive words to soften the tone and make the idea more palatable. You may even need to take a few more words, but this does not excuse wordy or obscure sentences. Let's face it, a refusal is a refusal, and you only irritate your reader more if you are not concise.

A. Within the framework of present regulations, negative considerations appear upon careful consideration to be such as to render a favorable action upon the request of your recent letter impossible at this time.

B. I am sorry, but we cannot approve your request.

Which of these is more courteous? _____

B ("Within the framework of present regulations" and "at this time" are really insincere because they imply that something—a revolution presumably—will come along to reopen the whole case.)

26a Remember that even though you choose a positive word, you can't always be certain of getting a pleasant overtone. The reader's final impression will depend not only on the word you choose, but on how you use it.

For instance:

I am patiently waiting to hear from you.

By itself, "patiently" is a/an _____ word.

---

positive

26b In the above sentence, would the reader get the impression that the writer was in fact "waiting patiently"? _____

No (You can almost see the writer tapping his foot with *im*patience.)

27 One final point: In your efforts to use positive, friendly, and courteous words, do not go to the opposite extreme. It might be as antagonizing as the cold, impolite letter.

Mr. and Mrs. Alfred C. Carey
12 Wyman Street
Libertyville, Massachusetts 01054

Dear Mr. and Mrs. Carey:

As you know, we're pretty proud of the fine service we offer here at Regent Diaper Service, Inc. And we always keep a sharp eye out for new folks who will benefit from the service our customers have, over the years, learned to expect from us.

That's why we took great pleasure in hearing about a potential shipping clerk who might be interested in a job, say around the year 1990 . . . name of Alfred Carey, Jr.

He's a bit small to be interviewed as yet, but tell him to drop in at his earliest convenience, won't you? We'll be delighted to make his acquaintance.

In the meantime, please accept our heartiest congratulations on the new arrival! We know that he'll grow up to be as fine a man—and shipping clerk—as his father.

Enclosed is our brochure with a detailed description of our services and rates.

Sincerely,

Is this letter likely to have the effect that the writer intended?_____

No (Please, no love, no kisses—just polite and courteous letters. Don't be coy, cute, or folksy. Don't snuggle up to the reader. This letter makes all the mistakes from false enthusiasm to mistaken assumptions. Does the letter writer *know* that the Careys want their son to be a shipping clerk?)

Don't forget your reader

One fault characterizes business writers above all others: a failure to remember the reader. The collection agent for a furniture store learned this when he sent the following letter to a late-payor:

> Dear Mr. Smith:
>
>   What will your neighbors think if we have to send our truck out to your house to repossess that furniture on which you have not met your last three payments?
>
> Sincerely yours,
The Acme Furniture Co.

A week later he received this answer:

> Dear Sirs:
>
>   I have discussed the matter you wrote me about with all my neighbors and every one of them thinks it would be a mean, low-down trick.
>
> Yours truly,
John Smith

Robert L. Shurter, *Written Communication in Business*

Now begin the exercises.

EXERCISES

Use your mask here.

A Rewrite the following sentences so that they are natural, friendly, and courteous.

1 Send your payment for $1.64 immediately, and then your receipt will be mailed to you.

You should have . . .

1 Inserted "please"
2 Omitted "immediately" or repositioned it in the second main statement
3 Made "receipt will be mailed" active

> Please send us your payment for $1.64 and we will immediately mail your receipt to you.

2 Advise us whether the Knightsbridge Street address, as shown above, is incorrect or not.

You should have . . .

1 Inserted "please" or turned the sentence into a question
2 Deflated "advise"
3 Omitted "as shown above"
4 Used "correct" in place of "incorrect"

Would you let us know whether the Knightsbridge Street address is correct?

or

Please tell us whether the Knightsbridge Street address is correct.

3   Since you claim you have lost your license, we are sending a form to complete for the issuance of a duplicate license.

You should have . . .

1   Omitted the first clause
2   Turned "issuance" into an action verb
3   Written a courteous request for action

>   Please complete this form so that we can issue you a duplicate license.

4   If you neglect to return the dividend request form, the dividends will not be forwarded to you.

You should have . . .

1   Made the first clause positive
2   Made "will not be forwarded" positive

>   If you send us the dividend request form, we will send (forward) your dividends to you.

5   Since you have abandoned the plan to increase the amount of your loan, I no longer need the contract and am returning it to you.

You should have . . .

1   Used a less negative word than "abandoned"
2   Omitted "the amount of"
3   Omitted "I no longer need"

>   Since you have decided not to increase your loan, I am returning your contract to you.

6   This oversight on your part can be remedied, since you still have thirty days to make payment.

You should have omitted "this oversight on your part can be remedied."

>   You still have thirty days to make payment.

7   Your letter with an explanation of your delinquency has finally arrived.

You should have . . .

1   Omitted "delinquency"
2   Omitted "finally"

> Thank you for your letter of explanation.
>
> or
>
> Your letter of explanation arrived.

8   I request that you mail the application promptly to me.

You should have . . .

1   Deflated "I request"
2   Used a softer word than "promptly"

> May I have the application (as) soon (as possible)?
>
> or
>
> Please mail the application (as) soon (as possible).

9   It is inconceivable that you didn't realize that the interest was due on June 15.

You should have replaced "it is inconceivable" with "perhaps" or "maybe."

> Perhaps you didn't realize that the interest was due on June 15.

10   We must deny payment of your claim inasmuch as the injury you claim benefits for did not really disable you nor prevent you from returning to work on the same day you received your injury.

You should have . . .

1   Softened "we must deny"
2   Replaced "inasmuch as" with "because" or "since"
3   Omitted "did not really disable you"

> I'm sorry that we cannot allow benefits on your claim, because your injury did not prevent you from returning to work on the same day you received it.
>
> or
>
> Since you returned to work on the same day that you received your injury, I'm sorry that we cannot allow benefits on your claim.

B   Rewrite the following letter sentence by sentence so that it becomes natural, friendly, and courteous.

> Dear Mr. Ford:
>
> 1 No record of your remittance for the February bill which you claim was paid has been found.   2 We are unable to report this as paid.   3 When your canceled checks are returned, should it occur that there is one among them endorsed by us, please forward same, and we will once again look into the matter.
>
> Sincerely yours,

> 1 I'm sorry, but we can't find a record of your payment for your February bill.

You should have . . .

1   Made the sentence active

2 Deflated "remittance"
3 Omitted "which you claim was paid"

> 2 **You should have omitted this sentence.**

> 3 When your canceled checks are returned, will you look for the check representing this payment? If you will send it to us, we will be happy to mark this bill "paid."

You should have . . .

1 Shortened and simplified "should it occur that there is one among them endorsed by us"
2 Deflated "please forward same"
3 Written something more specific than " we will once again look into the matter"

HELPFUL HINT

After you write the first draft of your next letter, look at each word by itself. Count the number of negative words. If you find more than two or three, your letter may not have a friendly tone. Perhaps you can soften your tone by using more positive or neutral words.

"Notice how the tone of your correspondence changes right after you've had your lunch, Mr. Dewlap?"

Reprinted from *The Wall Street Journal.*

THIRTEEN

BE PERSONAL

Be sure that you know what your correspondent is asking before you begin to answer him. Study his letter carefully. If he is obscure, spare no trouble in trying to get at his meaning. If you conclude that he means something different from what he says (as he well may), address yourself to his meaning, not to his words, and do not be clever at his expense.

Get into his skin, and adapt the atmosphere of your letter to suit that of his. If he is troubled, be sympathetic. If he is rude, be specially courteous. If he is muddle-headed, be specially lucid. If he is pig-headed, be patient. If he is helpful, be appreciative. If he convicts you of a mistake, acknowledge it freely and even with gratitude. But never let a flavour of the patronising creep in.

Sir Ernest Gowers

Use your mask here.

1 A pleasant tone can be achieved if you are natural, friendly, and courteous. In addition, your letter should also be *personal*. Through your language, your letter should show your reader that you think of him not as a statistic, but as a person. And it should prove that you are a person too—and not a mere cog in the organizational machinery.

Personal business letters are good public relations. For public relations is no more or less than the cumulative effect of a number of individual relations. If you write with a style that expresses your personality, your readers will be confident that they are receiving personal attention, and many of these individual relations will flourish.

However, if your letters have that impersonal, mass-produced look, the reader may not feel that the organization is genuinely concerned with his problems.

Which of the following is more personal?

A. Your contract is still in force. Our notice telling you it had lapsed was intended for another contract-owner. I'm sorry for any inconvenience our notice might have caused you.

B. A notice was sent to the above address advising of a lapse of contract. However, this notice was intended for another contract-owner. It should be disregarded.

A (From paragraph A, the reader can tell that an individual human being wrote it. Also, he can tell that the writer was thinking of him when he wrote it. In paragraph B, however, notice how all mention of the reader has been studiously avoided. The reader gets no idea that there's anyone behind the words, saying them.)

THE "YOU" ATTITUDE

2 One very effective device for being personal is to emphasize the "you" attitude. When you can, talk about the reader and his interests, not about yourself or your organization's interests.

Read this sentence:

I'm always glad whenever anybody asks me to explain the Ilex Computing System.

Notice how all mention of the reader has been avoided. "Anybody" is particularly impersonal. The reader may feel "Well, *I'm* not anybody." Rewrite this with the "you" approach. _____

I'm happy to answer *your* question(s) about the Ilex Computing System.

or

Thank *you* for *your* interest in the Ilex Computing System.

or

I'm happy to explain the Ilex Computing System to *you.*

3 Here's a sentence from a letter written to a student who's considering accounting as a profession.

The enclosed pamphlet—one of a series we are publishing on careers for young people—covers the accounting profession.

This is not terribly objectionable, but the student might be more impressed if we played down the emphasis on "we" and "the company." The reader is not primarily interested in the company's publishing activities. He's interested in *himself*. Rewrite this sentence, emphasizing the "you" attitude. _____

Here is a pamphlet which will help *you* make your decision about the accounting profession.

or

The enclosed pamphlet—one of a series we are publishing on careers for young people like *yourself*—will help *you* decide about the accounting profession.

4

It has been a pleasure to work mutually on this project.

Make this courtesy more personal. _____

I have enjoyed working with *you* on this project.

or

It has been a pleasure to work with *you* on this project.

5

I'm glad to hear of your decision, and I feel that, by following my outlined suggestions, the best possible course of action has been chosen.

Stop congratulating yourself and congratulate the reader. Make this more concise and personal. _____

You are correct if you . . .

1 Omitted the dangling participle
2 Made the second main statement active

I think that *you* have chosen the best possible course of action.

or

I think *you* will be happy with *your* decision.

6

The dividends can be left to the credit of your account or withdrawn.

This needs more "you." Rewrite it. _____

You can leave the dividends to be credited to your account, or *you* can withdraw them.

THE USE OF "I"

7 Another way to be more personal is to make the reader aware of you, the writer, by using "I."

It was felt that an immediate halt to construction activity would prevent further loss.

If this means, "I thought . . . ," say so. It's more personal. Also, this effort to avoid "I" will force you to use too many passive sentences. In fact, some writers will go to any extent to avoid identifying themselves directly with the reader. Notice how old-fashioned the following is.

This writer assures you that . . .

Rewrite this. _____

I assure you that . . .

8 Look for opportunities to show your reader that you know *he* is there by using "_____." Occasionally, when it seems natural, use "_____."

---

you
I

THE USE OF "WE"

9 Sometimes, "we" is more appropriate than "I." Generally, use "I" when you are speaking for yourself. Use "we" when speaking for your organization or for several people within it.

    A. I was very interested in your proposal. I showed it to the two other members of the department, and together, _____ decided to do what you ask.

    B. I was very interested in your proposal. May _____ suggest that you let me look at it again in a few months?

    C. I am sorry that we cannot meet your request, but _____ give refunds only within ten days after the date of sale.

    A. we
    B. I
    C. we

10 Which is more appropriate here, "I" or "we"? _____

I have studied your proposal carefully. You will understand, _____ know, that . . .

I

11 Which of these seems more sincere? _____

    A. I am glad to send you this check for $24.50.
    B. We are glad to send you this check for $24.50.

A (It's a little difficult for a reader to believe that the company is glad. Companies don't have emotions or opinions. However, if there *were* several people involved in sending the check and if the reader knows this, then "we" is appropriate.)

12 The owner of an appliance store in County Seat, Wyoming, receives a letter from a rural housewife telling him how much she likes the new blender he sold her two weeks ago. Here is his answer:

> Dear Mrs. Montgomery:
>
> We received your thoughtful letter and we wish to state how grateful we are for your expression of confidence in our new blender.
>
> Our wish has always been that we should be of service to our customers if they need us.
>
> Sincerely yours,

The emphasis is all wrong here. It needs more "you" and "I." Rewrite the letter. You can make any kinds of changes that you wish. _____

You are correct if you . . .
1 Used "I" in place of "we"
2 Inserted two or three "you's"

> Dear Mrs. Montgomery:
>
> Thank *you* for *your* thoughtful letter. It was kind of *you* to take the time to tell *me* how pleased *you* are with *your* new blender.
>
> If *you* should ever want to call on *me* again, *I'll* be happy to serve *you*.

It may be the official policy in your company to avoid "I," "we," and "you"—although resistance is crumbling. In any case, you still owe it to your reader to use specific, concrete words in sentences designed to fit *his* situation, and his alone. If you do, your reader will know that you are *personally* concerned with his problems and interests, and you think of him as an individual human being.

Now begin the exercises.

EXERCISES

Use your mask here.
A Give the following sentences a more pleasant tone by making them more natural, friendly, courteous, and personal. Concentrate on giving the proper emphasis to "I," "you," and "we."

1 If this change is desired, it would be necessary that the attached form be signed and dated.

You should have . . .
1 Deflated "desired"
2 Used "you" as the subject of the "if" clause
3 Omitted "it would be necessary"

> If *you* want this change, please sign and date this form.

2 It is a pleasure to send this check.

You should have . . .

1 Inserted a "you"
2 Used "I" as the subject. "We" is also acceptable, although it's harder to believe that the company is pleased.

> *I* am (*we* are) pleased (glad, happy) to send *you* this check.

3 If an additional $100 is needed, the loan can be increased.

You should have . . .

1 Made both the clause and the main statement active
2 Used "you" as the subject of the clause
3 Used "we" or "you" as the subject of the main statement. You might also use "I" in the rare case when the writer himself would be performing the actions of increasing the loan

> If *you* need an additional $100, *we* (*you, I*) can increase your loan.

4 We want to give the assurance that your request will be given immediate attention.

You should have . . .

1 Used "I" as the subject of the main statement. Usually, the company isn't doing the assuring; the writer is. You might use "we" in this case if you were speaking for several other people.
2 Inserted "you"
3 Made the clause active
4 Used "I" or "we" as the subject of the clause

> *I* (want to) assure *you* that *we* (*I*) will give your request immediate attention.

5 We are happy to be in a position to supply this information.

You should have . . .

1 Used "I" in place of "we." You would only use "we" in the rare case when you were writing for several other people.
2 Inserted "you"

> *I* am happy (to be able) to supply this information to *you*.

6 Enclosed will be found our General Office check.

You should have used "I" as the subject of the main statement.

> *I* am enclosing our General Office check.
>
> or
>
> *I* am glad to send *you* our General Office check.

7 As soon as we receive this form, this change will be effected.

You should have . . .

1   Made "I" or "we" the subject of the main statement. "I" is appropriate if the writer plans to make the change himself. "We" is appropriate if the writer expects someone else to make the change.
2   Deflated "effected"
3   Inserted "you" somewhere

> As soon as *we* receive this form, *we* (*I*) will make this change for *you.*

8   It is not quite certain to me as to what was desired in your request.

You should have . . .

1   Used "I" as the subject of the main statement
2   Used "you" as the subject of the clause
3   Deflated "desired"

> *I* was not quite certain (sure) what *you* wanted.

9   We're sorry this happened.

> *I'm* sorry this happened. (Usually, the writer is the only one that is "sorry." Sometimes, of course, there may be several people involved, and if you're speaking for them, then "We're sorry" is appropriate.)

10   It would be very convenient for me to make our appointment at 10 A.M. on June 11 at the Home Office.

> Would it be convenient for *you* to meet with *me* at 10 A.M. on June 11 at the Home Office?

HELPFUL HINT

After you write your next letter, test your "I's," "you's," and "we's." See if you can add a few "you's." Make sure that you have used "I" and "we" apropriately.

PART THREE
PLANNING AND WRITING LETTERS

This part deals with the actual writing of letters—with particular emphasis on making them well organized.

FOURTEEN
WRITE EFFECTIVE BEGINNINGS AND ENDINGS

College graduates need considerable practice in organizing and in presenting simply the more complex ideas they work with daily. This need is particularly felt in the more technical groups—scientists, engineers, and the like.

George F. Smith, President, Johnson & Johnson

Use your mask here.

BEGINNINGS

1a Every salesman knows that the first impression he makes on the potential customer is extremely important. Everything that follows builds from the opening. In the same way, it is crucial to the success of your business letter that its opening sentence effectively set the stage for what is to follow.

Because of his natural curiosity, the reader will read your first sentence with interest. But if your opening is clumsy or ineffective, his interest may be dissipated.

One of the best ways to lose a reader right away is to ease into the letter with a cliché warmup. Many business writers find it difficult to get started, so they perform a sort of verbal exercise before they let their reader know what they're writing to him about.

Which of the following do you recognize as a cliché warmup? _____

    A. This is in answer to your letter of July 15.
    B. I think I'll be able to answer all the questions in your letter of July 15.

A (Because sentence A tells the reader nothing he cares about, his interest is not captured. Sentence B, however, is much more likely to interest the reader because it tells him what the letter is about.)

1b Here are the opening sentences from three different letters. Which one will more likely capture the reader's interest? _____

    A. Yours of the 17 received and noted.
    B. If you will fill in the enclosed form, we'll be happy to send you our monthly bulletins on industrial training developments.
    C. We received your inquiry of November 6.

B (Openings A and C do tell the reader that the letter is about some letter he sent, but they don't tell him enough. He may have sent several letters on the date specified, and he still may not know what the *writer's* letter is about. Opening B not only tells the reader that the letter is about industrial training but also tells him the point of the whole letter. The reader is now ready for the writer to expand whatever he has to say.)

WHAT THE LETTER IS ABOUT

2 The first question your reader wants answered when he opens your letter is "What is this about?" Thus, your opening sentence should always answer this question—with the occasional exception of the teaser opening in a sales letter, as in: "It's springtime again—time to start making plans for the hot summer months ahead."

You are the credit manager of a department store to which Mr. Howard Astor has applied for a charge account. You are writing to an officer of Mr. Astor's bank, where he maintains a checking account, to get his credit rating. Remember: immediately tell the officer what you are writing to him about. Write your opening sentence.

Dear Mr. Morgan:

_____

You are correct if you started right out by telling the reader that you want Mr. Astor's credit rating. You are incorrect if you started by telling the reader that Mr. Astor has applied for a charge account. To this, the reader's reaction might well be, "so what?" He needs to know *what* **you're writing about before he knows** *why* **you're writing.**

> Could you please give me the credit rating of Mr. Howard Astor who maintains a checking account with your branch?
>
> or
>
> I would like to have the credit rating of Mr. Howard Astor, who maintains a checking account with your bank.

3 There is, of course, no reason why you shouldn't tell your reader in your opening sentence why you're writing him, but it's imperative that you tell him what your letter is about.

You are chief accountant in the accounts receivable department of a large publishing company. You find that Public School 28 has not paid its bill for one hundred *Physics in Action* textbooks which your company shipped two months ago. You're writing the principal a reminder. What is your opening? _____

_____

You are correct if the principal can tell from your sentence that you are writing about his delay in paying for the textbooks.

> This is just a reminder that we have not yet received payment of your order for one hundred *Physics in Action* textbooks.

4 Below are four openings to four different letters. Which one or ones tell the reader what the letter is about? _____

> A. I am sorry but we cannot do as you asked.
> B. We at Regent Investment Company, Inc. would like to invite you and your wife to be our guests at the Netherlands Hotel for a slide lecture on our latest real estate offerings for summer homes in Glen Lake, Virginia.
> C. We at Townton General Stores, Inc. have been in the hardware business for some twenty years.
> D. We are proud to announce the grand opening of our newest Red Star dairy and produce store on South and Vine Streets.

B and D

THE IDEA OF MOST INTEREST TO THE READER

5 The letters you send will contain information that the reader considers as positive, neutral, or negative news. In the first two instances (we'll talk about negative letters later), the ideas can be divided into two categories: those things you, the writer, are interested in, and those things your reader is interested in. So, when you select the ideas for your opening sentence, tell the reader what you're writing about *and*, if you can, include the idea which will most interest *him*.

Every reader wants to know immediately, "What is this about?" But he also wants to know something equally important. He wants to know, _____

A.   "How can I be of help?"
B.   "How can this help me?"

B

6

Dear Mr. Royster:

In a few days you will hear from the Tulsa office, which carries the records of your investment holdings. One of our representatives will visit your house with a check for $33,000, the face value of your bonds, which, I'm pleased to tell you, will mature on November 8.

Sincerely,

Notice how the pot of gold has been saved to the end. It does not belong there. Rewrite the opening sentence so that it contains the most important idea of interest to the reader. _____

I'm pleased to tell you that your bond investments will mature November 8.
or
I'm pleased to tell you that our representative will deliver $33,000 to you when your bond investments mature November 8. (Thus, in addition to telling your reader what your letter is about, your opening sentence should often include the idea which will most interest your *reader*.)

7   You're a social psychologist for a market research firm, and you're sending a lengthy questionnaire to selected housewives in order to measure their opinions and attitudes about a new cosmetic called Lip Stick. To gain the cooperation of your reader, you enclose a letter of explanation with an offer to send each woman a free sample of Lip Stick when she fills in and returns the questionnaire. You are interested in your reader filling in and returning the questionnaire. Your reader says, "What's in it for me?" Write your opening sentence. _____

You are correct if your sentence tells the reader that the letter is about filling in the Lip Stick questionnaire and also offers her the free sample.

You can receive a free sample of Lip Stick by filling in the enclosed questionnaire and returning it to us.

8   You are the president of Spinning Speed, Inc., a manufacturer of speedome-

ters. You are planning to build a new plant outside of town, and you are writing to various construction companies asking them to send bids for the job. Write your opening sentence.

Gentlemen:

_____

You are correct if your sentence tells your readers that the letter is about your plans to build a new plant and if it tells them that you are seeking bids for the job.

We're planning to build a new plant outside of town, so if you're interested, we'd like to have you bid for the job.

9   What should the opening sentence of your letter *always* tell the reader?

_____

What else should you try to include as often as possible in your opening sentence? _____

What the letter is about.
The idea that is most interesting (promises the most benefit) to the reader.

REFERENCE TO THE DATE

10   It is common practice, when replying to a letter, for the business writer to refer to the date of that letter in his opening sentence. For example:

In your letter of June 10, you asked . . .
Your assumption, in your letter of February 9, is correct.

By referring to the date of the reader's letter like this, you help to *identify* that letter for him. Most likely, if you're writing to someone in an organization, he is a busy person who sends many letters. If he has the date of the letter he sent you, he can quickly look it up in his files.

But reference to the date of your reader's letter should never become an excuse for a cliché warmup. Always talk immediately about the business at hand. When you refer directly to the date of your reader's letter, *subordinate* the idea. Don't make a main statement of it.

Which of the following is the best way to include reference to the date of your reader's letter? _____

A.   This is in reply to your letter, dated June 2.
B.   Thank you for your interest in our missile program, expressed in your letter of June 2.
C.   We are in receipt of your letter of June 2.

B

11

Dear Mr. Apdecker:

We received your letter of August 29. Here is pamphlet 518, *The Care and Feeding of Chicks*, which you asked for.

Reference to Mr. Apdecker's letter has not been subordinated in the opening sentence. Revise this opening. _____

You are correct if you placed the reference to the reader's letter in a modifying clause or phrase.

Here is Pamphlet 518, *The Care and Feeding of Chicks*, which you asked for in *your letter of August 29.*

12

Mr. Harry Calvin
Peabody, Schenley, and Rhoder
509 Rushing Boulevard
Denver, Colorado 80215

Dear Mr. Calvin:

We received your latest letter, dated March 28. You are correct in assuming that the court has no legal jurisdiction in the Burke case.

Mr. Calvin seems to be a busy lawyer. It is necessary to identify the letter in which he made his assumptions. But a whole sentence devoted to this is wasteful. Rewrite it. _____

You are correct if you combined both sentences by placing the reference to the date of the reader's letter in a modifying clause or phrase.

In your letter of March 28, you were correct in assuming that the court has no legal jurisdiction in the Burke case.

CLICHÉ ENDINGS

13a   All business writers are tempted, occasionally, to slip in a cliché warmup. But it's at the end, when we sign off, that the parade of clichés begins. Look at the following:

Do not hesitate to call on us if we may be of further service.

Hoping to hear from you at your earliest convenience, I remain . . .

It has been a pleasure to be of assistance.

May we again thank you for your cooperation.

If you have seen many business letters, you probably have seen many cliché endings such as those above. They continue to thrive because they are formulas—

they require little time and thought. However, they rarely seem sincere, even though a writer who uses them may *be* sincere. The reader usually does not think so, because he's seen them so often.

Replace the following inflated, timeworn expression with a simple, conversational sentence. _____

Do not hesitate to call on us if we may be of further service.

You are correct if your revision omits "do not hesitate" and "further service."

Just give us a call if we can do anything more to help.

or

Let me know if I can further assist you.

13b Even though these revisions are conversational, they are likely to become clichés through constant use. To improve them further, refer to something specific which has been mentioned in your letter. In this case, let's say that you have just filled an order for thirty cases of Trixie Paper Cups.

Just give us a call if we can do anything more to help.

Rewrite this with a *specific* reference to the paper cups. _____

Just give us a call if you need any more paper cups (Trixie Paper Cups).

BE SPECIFIC

14

Hoping to hear from you at your earliest convenience, I remain . . .

The above could be improved by making the closing *simple* and *specific*. Let's say that your letter asks about a delayed shipment. Rewrite the example. _____

You are correct if you included the specific words "shipment" or "order" in your answer.

May I hear soon about our shipment (order)?

or

As soon as possible, would you tell me when we can expect to receive this shipment (order)?

15 Here's another problem in closing sentences:

We regret that we do not have better news for you, but if in the future you feel we can be of further service to you, please do not hesitate to call upon us.

"Further service" is particularly annoying to the reader because the writer has been of no help at all. Notice, also, how formal "we regret" is. Why not, "I'm sorry"?

Rewrite this so that you state the sentiment simply and directly. _____

I'm sorry we do not have better news for you, but I hope we may be of service to (help you) you another time.

REQUESTS FOR ACTION GO AT THE END

16   Some writers think they are not being courteous until they tack on a cliché expression of courtesy. But such stale amenities are unnecessary. Your courtesy to your reader should be apparent in what you have already said, and in the way you said it. So if you have accomplished your objectives, and if you find yourself sitting crouched over your letter with nothing more to say, then say nothing. Just stop.

But when your letter has the objective of getting action from the reader, a good place to state your request for action is at the *end*.

Below are three out-of-order sentences from the same letter.

A.   To be on the safe side, may we ask you to send these forms by October 25?

B.   These forms will enable you to obtain your loan in time to go on vacation on October 29 as you planned.

C.   After we have received these completed forms, it takes only two days to approve your loan.

Which of these sentences should come last? _____

A (It is the request for action.)

17   You are writing a letter to the personnel director of Ardcum Corporation to apply for the position of salesman. You state your experience and qualifications (things, presumably, that he is interested in). You know that he will probably be attending the Ardcum sales convention next week in your home town, Cleveland. It would be very convenient if you could get an interview with him at the convention. Write your final sentence—your request for action. _____

If your sentence has something like the following idea: "it would be very convenient for me if you would . . . ," you are incorrect.

If you are going to be attending the Ardcum sales convention next week, I wonder if I could see you there?

or

Could you give me an interview at the Ardcum sales convention next week?

18   You are a country doctor. Two weeks ago, you wrote to the Peabody Ethical Drug Company asking them to send you a research report titled, "The Effects of Mezomicin," by Dr. James M. Bender. You received, instead, sales literature promoting the drug. You're writing a second time. Write your closing sentence. _____

You are correct if your sentence is a request for action.

I do appreciate the sales literature you did send, but could you please send me the research report called "The Effects of Mezomicin," by Dr. James M. Bender?

USE THE LAST SENTENCE TO SUMMARIZE

19   The last sentence of your letter is also a good place to summarize, especially when your letter is long and complex. Summarizing gives special focus to your ideas and will help your reader remember your major points.

Which of the following is the more effective closing? _____

A.   It all boils down to this: Either you can put your money in a savings bank and be assured of at least 4½ percent annual interest payment, or you can invest in common stocks, which afford you an opportunity for higher returns but which also carry a higher risk.

B.   I hope you will give the above alternatives your careful consideration before making your decision.

A (Ending A is a very neat summary of the main ideas of the letter. Ending B is all right, but it is not a summary.)

20   Let's quickly review.

Your opening sentence should *always* tell your reader _____ .

what your letter is about

21   As often as possible, you should include in your opening sentence the idea which will be of most interest to _____

the *reader*

22   The last sentence of your letter is a good place to make a _____ or _____ .

a summary
a request for action

Now begin the exercises.

EXERCISES

Use your mask here.

A   Rewrite the following opening sentences.

1   I am most pleased to reply to your letter of March 6. Here is the information you asked for.

You are correct if you . . .

1   Combined both sentences and placed the reference to the date in a modifying clause or phrase
2   Deflated "I am most pleased"

I'm glad to give you the information you asked for in your letter of March 6.

or

Here is the information you asked for in your letter of March 6.

2 We wish to acknowledge your check in the amount of $46.54.

You are correct if you . . .
1 Thanked the reader for the check
2 Shortened "in the amount of"

> Thank you for your check for $46.54.

3 It is always a pleasure to be a bearer of good tidings. For your long and loyal patronage, you have been given a **5 percent discount**.

You are correct if the reader finds out about his discount in the first sentence.

> (I am happy to tell you that) We are giving you a 5 percent discount for your long and loyal patronage.

4 I have your letter of August 11 at hand. I just want to say that we can answer all your questions.

You are correct if you . . .
1 Combined the two sentences and placed the references to the date in a modifying clause or phrase
2 Omitted "at hand"

> I can answer all the questions you asked in your letter of August 11.

5 This is to inform you that we received your goods on December 1. But some of the dresses were soiled.

You are correct if you combined the sentences so your reader knows immediately what you are writing him about.

> Some of your dresses, which arrived on December 1, were soiled.
>
> or
>
> Your dresses arrived on December 1, but some of them were soiled.

B Rewrite the following endings.
1 If you have any questions, do not hesitate to contact us.

You are correct if you deflated "do not hesitate to contact us."

> If you have any questions, please let us (me) know (please call, write, etc.).

2 Thanking you in advance, I remain . . .

> Thank you.

3 Let me say again in closing that we hope you will give careful consideration to

our recommendations and that you will notify me of your decision as soon as possible.

You are correct if you . . .

1   Omitted "Let me say again in closing that we hope you will give careful consideration to our recommendations"
2   Deflated "notify"

> Will you tell us your decision soon?

4   I regret that I cannot fill your order now, but if I can be of further service at a later date, please let me know.

You are correct if you . . .

1   Deflated "I regret"
2   Omitted "further"
3   Deflated "at a later date"

> I am sorry we cannot fill your order now, but if I can serve you later, please let me know.

5   May we have your check before October 6? Thank you for your prompt attention to this matter.

You are correct if you eliminated the last sentence or if you just said "thank you."

> May we have your check before October 6? (Thank you.)

HELPFUL HINT

Test the beginning and ending sentences of your next letter by asking yourself the following questions.

1   Is my beginning a cliché warmup or does it tell the reader what my letter is about?
2   Have I placed the idea which will most interest the reader in my beginning sentence?
3   Is my closing sentence effective or is it just a meaningless cliché?

FIFTEEN
ORGANIZE YOUR THOUGHTS
BEFORE YOU WRITE

A military man who cannot issue orders that are understood by the troops would give his opponent an unusual advantage. And a business man without ability to express his intentions and reasons has an equal handicap.

George A. Spater, President, American Airlines

TIPS FOR PLANNING

A well-planned business letter depends on the clear thinking you do *before* you compose your first sentence. There are several things you can do beforehand to clarify your thinking:

Read and Reread Each Incoming Letter

If you answer a great many letters every day, you may read each letter only once before answering it. While the pressure of work occasionally makes this necessary, careful rereading of each letter will save you time eventually. Some of the incoming letters may be unclear. So if you carefully reread, your reply will be complete, and you won't risk having to write a follow-up.

Mark the Main Ideas of the Letter to be Answered

If you mark the main ideas of the letter to be answered, a quick glance will then give you some of the essential ideas around which you can organize your answer. And if you confine your reply to these ideas, your letter will be concise.

Get Background Information

Even when you aren't replying to a letter, it's always helpful to do a little research. Glance through any correspondence you may have had with the reader. Find out everything you can about him. The small amount of extra time you spend may mean the difference between a poor letter and a letter which is truly effective.

Sort Your Ideas

Once you've done the above to get started, look critically at the ideas you have in your head and at your fingertips. From them, choose only those that are relevant to the purpose of your letter and to the needs of your reader. You must *sort* the relevant ideas from the irrelevant ideas.

To show you how sorting works, we're going to show you a letter that is ineffective because the writer didn't properly sort his ideas. Remember, however, that you will normally sort *before* you write your letter, not afterward.

Here's the situation: Mr. Rose, a steelworker, had a heart attack. His doctor told him that he probably couldn't return to work for a year. During the sixth month of Mr. Rose's convalescence, he wrote his insurance company asking them to waive his monthly premium payments on his life insurance policy. He did this because the terms of the policy entitled him to skip payment after total disability of more than six months.

When the company received Mr. Rose's letter, they sent a form for him and his doctor to fill in. It was completed and returned to the company, which then decided in his favor and sent him the following letter to tell him the good news. This letter shows, in addition to the abuse of clarity, conciseness, and force, evidence that the writer did not *sort* the wheat from the chaff.

Use your mask here.

CLAIM-ADJUSTMENT LETTER—GOOD NEWS

July 10,
Policy 576-6137

Mr. Philias Rose
7 Dniper Road
Pittsburgh, Pennsylvania 15206

Dear Mr. Rose:

Regarding Form 310-D recently requested and received and properly completed with a view to our considering the waiver of premium payments under your policy, I am writing you.

As you are aware, an insured is allowed to apply for the waiver of premium benefit if he should become totally disabled. Your application was sent to our Medical Department which returned it to me.

Beginning with your July 5 premium payment for the above-numbered policy No. 576-6137, the company will waive payment. If your check for this payment has already been sent, a refund will be made in the near future.

As long as you remain totally disabled as defined in the policy, the Disability Benefit Provision will be in force. And if these conditions are maintained, the company will waive payment of future premiums as they fall due.

If you have any questions during your period of total disability, please let me know.

Sincerely,

1a Look at the *first sentence* of the letter. Forget, for a moment, how badly it is written and examine only the ideas expressed. You can see three ideas leading up to the word "with." The first tells Mr. Rose that Form 310-D was recently requested. Is Mr. Rose already aware that the form was "recently requested"? _____

Yes

1b Since Mr. Rose already knows this idea, it would be a good idea to sort it, to throw it out. The other two ideas tell Mr. Rose that Form 310-D was "received" and "properly completed." Is Mr. Rose already aware of this? _____

No

1c However, in a moment, you will see that you can tell Mr. Rose these facts without using words. But first look at the main statement, "I am writing you." What should be done with this? _____

Sort it out. Get rid of it.

1d There *is* some relevant meaning for Mr. Rose in what remains. After all, when a reader first opens a letter, he wants to know what it's about. Why not meet this need by *thanking* Mr. Rose for filling in the form, and at the same time, telling him what the letter is about by identifying the form as his request for waiver of his premium payment? Rewrite the opening sentence. _____

Thank you for filling in the form requesting a waiver of your premium payments. (Notice that this also tells Mr. Rose by implication that the form "was received" and "properly completed.")

1e Note the first sentence of the second paragraph. What should be done with this idea? _____

Sort it out. (It tells Mr. Rose something he already knows.)

1f Look at the second sentence in the second paragraph. Does the reader need this information? _____

No (He's not interested in office procedures.)

1g Look at the first sentence in the third paragraph. Does this sentence have some information that Mr. Rose needs? _____

Yes

1h This sentence tells Mr. Rose some very good news. Yet one part is completely unnecessary. What is it? _____

the above-numbered policy 576-6137 (The policy has already been identified at the top of the letter.)

1i Read the fourth paragraph. It attempts to present a line of reasoning, but has been cluttered with unnecessary repetition. What is necessary is the idea that total disability is the condition for continuing waiver of premiums. Complete the following by using relevant ideas only.

As long as _____, we will _____ .

As long as you are totally disabled as defined in your policy, we will continue to waive payment.

1j Note the last sentence. It is courteous, but even here, there is an unnecessary idea. Rewrite the sentence. _____

If you have any questions, please let me know.
or
Do you have any questions? If so, please let me know.

The revised letter now reads:

July 10,

Mr. Philias Rose
7 Dniper Road
Pittsburgh, Pennsylvania 15206   Policy 576-6137

Dear Mr. Rose:

Thank you for filling in the form requesting a waiver of your premium payments.

We have waived premiums on your policy beginning with your July payment. If you have already paid it, we'll refund it to you soon.

As long as you are totally disabled as defined in your policy, we will continue to waive payment.

Do you have any questions? If so, please let me know.

Sincerely,

Granted, we have spruced up the writing, but the real gain came about because we included and excluded ideas which the original writer failed to sort in the first place. (An alternative and perhaps better way of opening the above letter would be to eliminate the first sentence—thus putting the good news right at the beginning. Isn't good news what the reader is most interested in?)

ADJUSTMENT LETTER—NEUTRAL NEWS

2a Most letters require some sorting and planning before you begin to construct sentences.

Let's say you are the bookkeeper in Music Equipment Store, a retail shop for musical instruments. Mr. Clarence Bryan has sent you a check for $35 to pay his sixth monthly installment on his Elton Grand Piano. Eighteen installments remain to be paid. When you take out his file to record his payment, you find that his wife has already taken care of the March installment. He owes nothing until April 11. So you return his check with a letter of explanation.

Your first step in planning this letter is to sort the relevant ideas from the information we have given you. List the ideas you would include in your letter to Mr. Bryan. Don't worry about constructing sentences. Just jot down the ideas.

_____

Please resist the temptation to look at our answer before you write your own. That way you will obtain the most benefit from the lesson.

You should _not_ have the following ideas in your list . . .

1   This is your _sixth_ premium payment and you have eighteen to go.
2   We have checked our files and found . . .
3   You might include the amount of the check, but it's debatable whether this is really relevant.

If you included any of the these ideas in your jottings, cross them out.

Here is our list of ideas:

1   Thanks for check.
2   Payment for March installment for Elton Grand Piano.
3   Returning it.
4   Wife paid it.
5   Owe nothing until April 11.

2b Now that you've sorted the relevant ideas, examine your list and begin to think of the sentences you're going to write. Juggle the ideas around. Examine the relationships between them. Write your letter. _____

You are correct if . . .

1 Your opening sentence tells what the letter is about
2 You recognized that idea 4 is the reason for the action of idea 3

> Dear Mr. Bryan:
>
> **Tells what the letter is about**
>
> Thanks for sending your check for the March installment on your Elton Grand Piano. I am, however, returning your payment because your wife has already taken care of it.
>
> You are paid up until April 11.
>
> > Sincerely,

LETTER OF INQUIRY

3a Now let's try planning and writing a more complicated letter.

Here's the situation: You're the Manager of the Accounting and Central Filing Department of Redding Metal Parts, Inc., a manufacturer of small hardware items such as hinges, doorknobs, metal fasteners, and the like. These items are marketed to about 10,000 wholesalers and retailers in the surrounding area. One of the distinguishing characteristics of Redding Metal Parts is the prompt, individual attention that is given to all orders.

Over the past few years, the firm's sales have been growing steadily—with resulting increases in your hard-working staff. You're pretty proud of the manual paper-handling system you've set up to take care of more than 200,000 orders each year, but lately there have been signs that the system may not be doing as good a job as it should. Delays in filling and shipping orders have increased. The warehouse, which relies on your department to keep track of inventory, has reported an increasing number of items that were listed as in-stock but in fact were not. The production department has reported growing problems in scheduling production runs on some items, because production is not being given enough warning that such items are getting low in the warehouse. Consequently, stockouts are increasing. The situation has not reached the crisis stage yet, but there is some feeling that the rapid growth in sales has been a mixed blessing.

You've just returned from your weekly conference with the president of the firm, the vice president in charge of production, and the manager of the warehouse. All agreed that there is some cause for concern. The vice president suggested that a computerized data processing system may be the answer, and you have just been assigned the task of studying the feasibility of such a solution. Since no one in the firm knows very much about EDP (electronic data processing), you recommended that a consultant be hired as the first step in the feasibility study. You have been given two weeks to make your recommendations as to which consultant should be engaged.

You're now sitting down to write a letter of inquiry to a business acquaintance, Mr. Henry L. Armstrong, Vice President, Data Processing Center, Valley National Bank. His organization has an EDP system, you are on a first-name basis with him, and he knows a good deal about the operations of Redding Metal Parts, because his bank has made several substantial loans to your firm.

Generally, a letter of inquiry has the following ingredients:

1 A clear statement of what is wanted, including who wants it and why.
2 A list of questions or a reference to an enclosed questionnaire.
3 An expression of appreciation.

Basically, a letter of inquiry asks the reader to do the writer a favor. Thus, you should ask as few questions as possible and make them clear, direct, and easy to answer.

Now let's get started on planning your letter. First, you should decide what your objective or objectives are. Which of the following do you think should be the objectives of your letter to Mr. Armstrong? _____

A. To explain in detail the history of your firm and how it operates.
B. To explain in detail the operational difficulties your firm is experiencing.
C. To mention your concern with operations, briefly and in general.
D. To obtain the name or names of reputable EDP consultants and Mr. Armstrong's opinion as to which may be best for your firm.
E. To find out if Mr. Armstrong believes that an EDP system would effect savings in operating costs.
F. To find out what the going rate for EDP consultants is.
G. To discover what personnel and training problems arise when an EDP system is installed.

C, D, F (Since Mr. Armstrong already knows about your firm, objective A would not be necessary. Objective B is not really warranted since it is usually not wise to allow outsiders to know too specifically what your problems are. Objective C is preferable, since it does require you to explain why you are writing. Objective D is, of course, essential if you are to accomplish your assignment. Objective E would be better answered by the consultant, not Mr. Armstrong. Objective F is sensible, since this information will be useful when negotiating for the consultant's services. Like objective E, objective G should be saved for the consultant.)

3b Now jot down the ideas you are going to include in your letter. Remember to sort out those that don't belong. You need not write full sentences. _____

Please don't look at our answer before you write your own.

1 We're thinking of EDP to solve some operating problems.
2 Want your advice.
3 Specifically, we want names of consultants.
4 What's the going rate?
5 Thanks.

3c Now that you know pretty much what you want to say, write your letter to Mr. Armstrong. _____

Again, please don't peek.

Mr. Henry L. Armstrong
Vice President
Data Processing Center
Valley National Bank

Dear Henry:

Tells what the letter is about
I wonder if you could give me some advice about hiring an EDP consultant. We are seriously considering the idea of installing an EDP system in our Accounting and Central Filing Department (**Tells why the information is needed**), to improve inventory control and provide better information for production scheduling.

Inquiries
Since no one here knows very much about EDP, could you give me some names of reputable consultants in the field to help us with our feasibility study? Also, I'd like to obtain some idea of what the going rates for such services are.

Expression of appreciation
I certainly appreciate any help you can give me with this. Thanks very much.

Sincerely,

Now begin the exercises.

EXERCISES

Use your mask here.

A Here's the situation: You're a correspondent for an insurance company. You receive the following letter.

Dear Sirs:

The factory here has been laying off a lot of men, and work is hard to come by. I need to borrow some money to get my family through this layoff, but the only way I know is to use my life insurance money. I think my policy is worth about $2,000, so could you send the money right away?

Sincerely yours,

Alex Lehmann

From the letter, you can't be certain whether Mr. Lehmann wants to borrow some money on his policy or to surrender it by taking the entire cash value. Both are possible. You look at Mr. Lehmann's file and find that the cash value (the amount he receives if he surrenders the policy) is indeed $2,000. You know that the loan value (the amount he can borrow on his policy) is $2,000—exactly the same amount.

You think that Mr. Lehmann should take a loan for several reasons. First of all, he will be able to meet his financial needs without entirely losing his valuable insurance protection. Secondly, if he should surrender his policy entirely and decide to apply for a new policy later on, he would have to pass another medical examination And of course the company benefits because it does not lose the customer.

Whenever a policy owner wants to withdraw money, he must fill in a form. To make sure you don't send him the wrong one, you decide to send him two forms. And you write a letter urging him to take a loan.

Jot down your ideas. Don't worry about constructing sentences yet.

Your list should not have any statements like . . .
1   "I was confused by your letter."
2   "Your letter was not clear."
3   "If you take a loan, we don't lose a customer."
4   "You can plainly see that . . ."
5   "I've looked at your files . . ."

Here are our jottings:

1   Glad to help when I know what you want.
2   Do you want us to pay the cash value?
3   Do you want us to give you a loan?
4   I don't want to send the wrong form.
5   Am sending both.
6   The cash value is $2,000.
7   The loan value is the same as the cash value.
8   Better to take a loan.
9   You'll probably meet your financial needs without entirely losing your valuable insurance protection.
10 You won't have to take a medical exam if you decide to apply for insurance protection later on.
11 Tell us your decision by filling out one of the two forms.
12 We'll be happy to help you.

Now think of the sentences you're going to write. How are you going to group your ideas in paragraphs? Are the ideas in the most logical order? Perhaps you better split some ideas in two sentences? Or maybe combine some. How about linking? Make sure all relationships are indicated for your reader. Now write your first-draft letter. _____

Take a five-minute break. Then come back to your letter and polish it. When you're satisfied that you've made it as effective as possible, check your letter with ours.

Dear Mr. Lehmann:

Tells what the letter is about

I will be happy to help you as soon as I am sure whether you want to surrender your policy or make a loan. Because I don't want to send you the wrong form for getting your money, I'm sending you both.

The cash value of your policy is $2,000 and the loan value is $2,000—exactly the same as the cash value. **(Suggestion and reasons for suggestion)** I suggest that you take a loan because you will probably meet your financial needs without entirely losing your valuable insurance protection. And you won't have to pass another medical examination if you decide to again apply for full insurance protection.

Request for action

You can tell us what you would like to do by filling in one of the two forms and sending it to us. We'll be glad to help you.

Sincerely,

HELPFUL HINT

Before you write your next letter, do the following:

1 Read carefully the letter you have received.
2 Underline the points you wish to cover.
3 Get all the background.
4 Jot down your ideas and *sort* them.
5 Think about these ideas and plan your sentences.

Then write your letter.

SIXTEEN
BE REASONABLE WHEN SAYING NO

No piece of company business can begin, progress, and achieve its purpose without the use of words. Writing, together with reading, is as much an integral part of business as your bones are part of your body.

Everyday in the future you will be called upon to speak and write, and when you open your mouth, or write a letter or report, you will be advertising your progress and your potential worth.

General Electric Company

Use your mask here.

1a It is usually much easier to say *yes* in a letter than to say *no*. For when you say *yes*, you are usually satisfying the reader. But when you say *no*, you must do it carefully and delicately, because no one likes to be turned down.

GIVE REASONS

The principles and techniques you use to make your business letters clear, concise, forceful, well organized, natural, friendly, courteous, and personal are especially pertinent when you sit down to write a letter which says *no*. For despite the negative situation, you must try to obtain or keep the goodwill of your reader.

Many business writing books say that every letter is a sales letter. But a turndown is, in addition, a salvage operation. For when you say no to a reader, you should also try to salvage his goodwill for your organization.

The first thing you can do to gain the reader's goodwill is to *give reasons for the turndown*, when possible. Your reader wants to know why his request has been refused. And nothing antagonizes him more than to be told only that the granting of his request is not in line with company practice.

Look at the following letter:

Mr. Kurt Jordan
Lukeville, Arizona 85341

Dear Mr. Jordan:

In your letter of December 12, you asked us to extend credit to you toward purchase of six big-game hunting rifles. However, it is not in line with company policy to do so.

We hope to have your cash order soon.

> Sincerely yours,

Has a satisfactory explanation been **p**rovided for the reader? _____

No (To make "company policy" the scapegoat is to make no explanation at all. The reader's comeback might be, "Well, *why* is company policy like that?")

1b Would you be inclined to send a cash order after receiving the above letter?

No (Many people wouldn't.)

1c Actually, the store has good reason for turning down Mr. Jordan's request for credit. It does not assume the risk of credit losses because it can then offer lower (more competitive) prices.

Rewrite the above letter with an explanation. Make sure your opening sentence tells the reader what the letter is about. State the reasons *first*, the actual refusal *second*. _____

Please resist the temptation to look at our answers before you write your own. That way you will obtain the most benefit from the lesson.

You are correct if . . .

1   Your opening sentence at least tells the reader what your letter is about
2   Your reasons follow the opening
3   The actual refusal follows your reasons
4   Your closing sentence is a request for action

> Dear Mr. Jordan:
>
> **Tells what letter is about**
> Thank you for your order of December 12 for six big-game hunting rifles. I am sure you noticed the lower prices at which we sell them. (**Reasons for turndown**) We can offer these bargains because we only allow cash purchases and therefore don't carry the added expense of credit transactions. (**Refusal**) So I hope you understand why we can only accept cash toward purchase of your rifles.
>
> **Request for action**
> May we have your check or money order soon?
>
> Sincerely,
>
> (You are also correct if you omitted the actual refusal. An implied refusal is all right, as long as there is no doubt that the letter is indeed a refusal. In the above case the intent of the letter remains intact without the refusal.)

Saying No to a Request

2a An appeal to the reader's most reasonable self will go a long way toward softening the shock of a refusal. By giving your reasons first, when you can, you make it easier for the reader to accept the actual turndown.

List your reasons courteously, simply, and clearly. Even when you are replying to an angry outburst, try to be tactful with the reader.

Below is a letter that deals with a very delicate situation. It is in reply to a reader who had written to her insurance company asking for a change-of-beneficiary form. Her husband, a captain in the Army, had asked her to change the beneficiary of his life insurance policy—just before she heard that he was missing in action. "There should be no difficulty," she had explained, "since I have power of attorney." The company had to say no. The first letter from the company brought an angry response that started, "I'm counting to ten as I write this," and ended with, "P.S. You're right I'm mad!"

This is the second refusal from the company:

Dear Mrs. Vansworth:

1   Please let me try to explain our position concerning your request to change the beneficiary on your husband's life insurance policy. To the lay person, power of attorney is an all-embracing instrument authorizing the agent to exercise and enjoy all the rights and privileges of the grantor. Unfortunately, this is not so. The rights of the attorney are specific and limited to the terms of the authorization. As a matter of fact, in your letter, you point out that the power of attorney filed with the Madison Insurance Company is an *insurance* power of attorney, and through it, you have encountered not the least difficulty. The power of attorney we have filed with us is a *general* power of attorney. Does this not suggest to you that the fault might lie in the inadequacy of the document itself rather than any lack of consideration on our part?

2   Nothing could be more apparent to us than Captain Vansworth's intention that you act for him in his absence. But our contract is with Captain Vansworth, and until he tells us otherwise, we're bound to protect his interest— right down to the small print! If you look on page two of the policy, you'll find that only the insured may change the beneficiary. That's a standard policy provision, one that you'll find in pretty nearly every life insurance policy issued in the United States. It's a very special right reserved to the insured alone because it is so vital to the control of the ownership of the policy, which is, in effect, personal property. When our Office of the General Counsel examined your power of attorney and found that this specific act was not explicitly stated, they had to suggest an alternative procedure.

3   But I have another suggestion that might work. Write to the Madison Insurance Company and ask them to send you a photostat of the insurance power of attorney in their file. When you receive it, read it carefully. If it isn't limited by its terms to the specific policy with their company, then by all means send it directly to me, and we will be glad to look it over.

4   I do hope I've been able to make our position clear, and that you no longer feel we acted arbitrarily. And may I send with this letter the sincere wish that your husband be returned very soon, safe and sound, to these shores.

Sincerely yours,

Look at the first paragraph. What does it do right away? _____

It starts explaining.

2b   Is the explanation general or specific? _____

specific

2c   Is the tone of the first paragraph reasonable or arbitrary? _____

reasonable

2d Notice the second paragraph. Does the opening sentence tell Mrs. Vansworth that her request is unreasonable? _____

No (On the contrary, it takes pains to recognize the validity of her request.)

2e In the rest of the second paragraph, the writer continues to give his detailed explanation. Does he ever appeal to "company policy"? _____

No

2f Notice the third paragraph. Does it look like the writer is going to back down and give in to Mrs. Vansworth? _____

No

2g Although the writer firmly maintains his position, he does offer Mrs. Vansworth an (alternative suggestion/apology). _____

alternative suggestion (He is trying to be helpful.)

2h Notice the final paragraph. Does it show the writer to be indifferent to or sympathetic with the reader's problem? _____

sympathetic with

2i Now look at the letter as a whole, and think of your total impression. Do you think Mrs. Vansworth's ruffled feathers were smoothed? _____

Yes (At least the writer can be sure he did everything possible to smooth them, short of granting her request.)

2j What do you think is the main reason for the probable success of this letter? _____

The writer provides a detailed explanation for the turndown. (If this had been done in the first letter, this expensive follow-up would not have been necessary.)

3 What is the most effective thing you can do to capture your reader's goodwill when you write a turndown? _____

Give an explanation for the turndown.

4 Generally, which should come first? The actual refusal or the explanation?

the explanation

Now begin the exercises.

EXERCISES

Use your mask here.

A In this exercise, you have only two turndown letters to write. So take your time.

As adjustor for the Bleakowen Department Store, you have received the following letter:

Gentlemen:

On March 26, I purchased a size fourteen tweed coat for my daughter in your Junior Miss Department. For this coat, which my daughter wanted for Easter, I paid $52.75.

One week after Easter, you advertised this same coat on sale in the *Morning Chronicle* for $29.95. It seems to me that it is outrageous for you to charge almost twenty-three dollars more for a coat just because it is purchased ten days before your sale, which I couldn't have known anything about. And anyway, we needed the coat for Easter.

I expect you to send me a credit slip for the difference in price. Otherwise I'll never do business with your store again.

Sincerely yours,

Mrs. J. E. Lewis

Your store policy is to grant such adjustments when the purchase takes place within the week preceding a special sale. However, Mrs. Lewis purchased the coat twelve days (almost two weeks) before the special sale. Also, holidays like Christmas and Easter are always followed by these sales. Your job is to write Mrs. Lewis and refuse the adjustment.

Remember, don't get mad at Mrs. Lewis. She's probably sitting at home right now and worrying that she may have taken too harsh a tone with you. Or maybe she just had something for breakfast that didn't agree with her on the morning she wrote her letter. By the time your letter arrives, we're sure that she'll be much more receptive to reason.

Now jot down the ideas you're going to include in your reply. What are you going to say in your opening sentence? Try to inject a note of sympathy or understanding. After you've jotted down your opening, what are you going to say? Should you state the refusal or leave it implied? Give a little thought to your closing sentence also. Once you've jotted down your ideas, sort them and compare your jottings with our jottings below. _____

We hope you didn't include ideas such as . . .

"Thank you for your letter . . ."

"You should have known that we always have sales after Easter."

"We regret to tell you . . ."

". . . the coat which is worth $52.75 and which is now selling for $29.95."

"It is not our policy to allow adjustments like yours."

"Perhaps you can take advantage of our policy in the future."

Here is our list:

1 I understand.
2 Let me explain.

3 Sales are customary after holidays.
4 Statement about our policy about such adjustments.
5 You bought the coat twelve days before the sale.
6 No credit on the difference in price. (Maybe this should only be implied?)
7 I hope you think this fair.
8 I hope we can continue to serve.
9 Note: be specific about daughter and tweed coat in opening sentence, but don't mention prices.

Now write your first draft. _____

Go back over what you wrote. Do you really want to say that? Polish your sentences. Read them aloud. Are you conversational? Friendly? When you think you have an effective letter, compare yours with our version.

Saying No to an Adjustment

Dear Mrs. Lewis:

Tells what the letter is about
I certainly understand how you must have felt when you saw the reduced price on your daughter's tweed coat in the *Morning Chronicle*. But may I explain?

Reasons for the refusal
Bleakowen's always offers sales after holidays such as Christmas and Easter, and we do allow adjustments such as yours when the purchase is made within the week before a special sale. Your purchase, however, was made twelve days before our sale. (**Refusal**) For this reason we cannot give you credit on the difference in price.

Courteous, optimistic close
I do hope that you will feel we have been fair and that we may continue to serve you.

Sincerely,

(Again, you are correct if you omitted the actual refusal, as long as you left no doubt in Mrs. Lewis's mind that she would not receive a credit.)

B You are the Safety Director of the Bureau of Motor Vehicles and Traffic Safety in Wheelersburg, a medium-sized city in Kentucky (zip code: 41473). Two weeks ago, you received a letter from a Mrs. Thornton Miller, a suburban resident, living at 156 Carnation Place. She asked that a traffic light be placed at the intersection of Carnation Place and Colton Avenue. She gave two reasons: (1) There have been five automobile accidents at that spot in the last two months. (2) The intersection is near a school, and the children need a light to help them cross the street. Enclosed with her letter was a petition signed by fifty other local mothers. When you received her letter, you sent an acknowledgment telling her that your traffic expert would study the problem.

His findings and recommendations were:

1   Traffic at the intersection is not heavy enough to warrant the expense of a light.
2   Stop signs are not properly placed and should be rearranged to greatly reduce the danger of car accidents.
3   A traffic policeman should be placed at the intersection when the children are going to and coming from school.

You accept these recommendations. You have the stop signs properly placed, and make arrangements with the Police Department for a policeman to be at the intersection between 8 and 9:30 A.M. when the kids go to school in the morning and between 3 and 4 P.M. when they go home.

Study the situation. Marshal your facts. Remember you have already written one letter to Mrs. Miller. Jot down your ideas and compare your jottings with ours below. _____

We hope you did not include ideas such as . . .

"Thank you for your letter . . ." (You already said that in your first letter to Mrs. M.)
"We had our traffic expert study the problem." (You already told her that, too.)

We also hope that you arranged your ideas so that you tell Mrs. Miller what you did do *before* you tell her what you didn't do

1   I know you're waiting for the report.
2   Our expert felt that there will be no more traffic accidents once the signs are moved.
3   We moved the signs.
4   Traffic cop between 8 and 9:30 A.M. and between 3 and 4 P.M.
5   This will keep the kids safe.
6   But you get no traffic light.
7   Not enough traffic and too expensive to taxpayers.
8   Thanks.
9   I like it when you're all conscious of traffic safety.
10 Note: be sure to thank the neighbors. She'll probably show the letter around.

Now write your first draft.

Hold it! Is that really the letter you want fifty or sixty civic-minded residents to read? They're going to give it a close going over. Have you done the same? When you're satisfied, compare your letter with the one below.

Saying No to a Request—2

Mrs. Thornton Miller
156 Carnation Place
Wheelersburg, Kentucky 41473

Dear Mrs. Miller:

Tells what the letter is about
I know you've been waiting to hear about our traffic expert's investigation of
the intersection at Carnation Place and Colton Avenue. He felt that the danger at this intersection could be largely removed if the stop signs were placed
in a better position. (**Tells what *was* done**) Acting on his recommendations, we
have rearranged the signs. Also, I am happy to say that a traffic policeman will

"Miss Pettifog, take a crank letter."

now be on duty at the intersection between 8 and 9:30 A.M. when the children go to school in the morning and between 3 and 4 P.M. when they return home in the afternoon. This will help ensure their safety.

Refusal and reason for refusal

Traffic at this intersection is light enough so that the expense to taxpayers of a traffic light can be saved. However, I am sure that the measures we have already taken will provide maximum safety for both children and drivers.

Courteous close

I do want to thank you and your neighbors for calling this to my attention. It is a pleasure to know that so many residents are alert to traffic safety problems in our city.

Sincerely,

HELPFUL HINT

The next time you write a turndown, ask yourself these two questions:

    Did I give a detailed, convincing explanation?
    Did I give reasons first and refusal second?

SEVENTEEN

TAKE A LITTLE LONGER

The manager has a specific tool: information. He does not "handle" people, he motivates, guides, organizes people to do their own work. His tool—his only tool—to do all this is the spoken or written word or the language of numbers. No matter whether the manager's job is engineering, accounting, or selling, his effectiveness depends on his ability to listen and to read, on his ability to speak and to write. He needs skill in getting his thinking across to other people.

Peter F. Drucker

Use your mask here.

ASSURE CAREFUL CONSIDERATION

1   In the preceding chapter, you learned to soften the blow of a refusal by giving *reasons* for it, generally *before* the actual refusal.

The following letter demonstrates an additional touch which helps to soften the blow. Notice how the first sentence assures the reader that his suggestion received careful consideration.

Dear Mr. Gordon:

We have carefully considered your suggestion that the M-15 accumulator be modified to your specifications. We think that these changes would certainly be well-received by our customers, but because of the expense involved, we will have to delay thinking about them seriously until next year.

Thanks for sending in your suggestion.

Sincerely,

Below is the opening sentence of another turndown letter. Rewrite it to make it more effective. _____

I received your application for admission to the Mechanical Engineering School.

I have carefully considered your application for admission to the Mechanical Engineering School.

2   But now consider this situation. Let's say that you're the manager of a store that never gives credit—to keep your prices as low as possible. You would, of course, give this as a reason for turning down any request for credit. However, the nature of your reason tells your reader that your refusal is a matter of policy and that the decision to refuse credit was made long before the reader's request was ever made. In this situation, would it be a good idea to tell the reader that his request received careful consideration?_____

No (He wouldn't believe you.)

GIVE POSITIVE ALTERNATIVES

3   Often, when denying a request, you can offer a positive alternative. Although many situations at first may seem totally negative, you can still be helpful by mentioning positive alternatives.

Here's such an opportunity: As correspondent for Images Limited, a photographic supplies wholesaler, acknowledge the first order from James Custer of the Flick Photo Shop, 311 Cody Street, Reno, Nevada 89504. The order is for:

1   2 movie projectors
2   1 enlarger
3   9 gallons of Prestone Developer

Item 1 has been shipped by highway truck express; item 2 is expected to be in stock within a week; and item 3 is not handled by Images but by the Photo Fluids Co., 1 Court Street, Wilmington, Delaware 19808.

Write your letter and play up the positive alternative. _____

Please resist the temptation to look at our answers before you write your own. That way you will obtain the most benefit from the lesson.

You are correct if you . . .

1 Told Custer what you did do before you told him what you couldn't do

2 Supplied him with a positive alternative by telling him where he could get his developer.

Saying No to a Request—3

Mr. James Custer
Flick Photo Shop
311 Cody Street
Reno, Nevada 89504

Dear Mr. Custer:

I'm happy to welcome you as a new customer to Images Limited. Thank you for your order.

The two movie projectors have been shipped by highway truck express, so you should receive them soon. We expect to have the enlarger in stock within a week and will ship it to you as soon as it arrives.

Unfortunately, we do not supply Prestone Developer, but you may obtain all you need from the Photo Fluids Co., 1 Court Street, Wilmington, Delaware 19808.

Sincerely,

USE NEUTRAL OR POSITIVE WORDS

4 In addition to giving positive alternatives, it is also important that you use words with neutral or pleasant overtones. Look at the following:

We are sorry that we are in no position to comply with your request.

This is a negative thought, granted, but doesn't the sentence sound unnecessarily arbitrary? See if you can soften the stiff tone. _____

You are correct if you used "I" in place of "we" and if you deflated "we are in no position to comply with your request."

I'm sorry that we cannot do as you ask.

Refusing a Payment

5

> We are herewith returning your check since we have been unable to apply these funds to your bill. Your bill was in the amount of $86.70, and your check was for $68.70. The reason for this may possibly be an inadvertent reversal of the figures on your part. We are sending the check back to you and await a new one.

This letter is negative and insulting. The request for action is rude. Rewrite it with neutral and positive words. _____

You are correct if you . . .

1 Deflated the language
2 Made a courteous request for action

> I am returning your check for $68.70 because your bill is for $86.70. Possibly you reversed the first two numerals. In any event, would you send us a new check for $86.70? Thank you.

6

> We are unable to accept the health certificate you recently forwarded to us since you neglected to sign it properly. Please date and sign the new certificate with your proper signature, "Adolph K. Compton."

This is unnecessarily negative. Rewrite it. _____

> Because we need your full signature, we are sending you another health certificate. Please date and sign it "Adolph K. Compton."
>
> or
>
> We need your full signature before we can accept your health certificate. Please date and sign the new one "Adolph K. Compton."

7a Readers like to know that their requests have received careful consideration. Even when they've been turned down, they often console themselves with the thought, "Well, at least they paid some attention to what I had to say."

Consequently, it's helpful to assure the reader of careful consideration. You can do this most effectively by using *specific* words which apply to his situation alone. For if you talk about the details of his problem, you have proved that you did more than just glance at his request.

Read the following letter which refuses credit to the reader. These letters are always difficult to write because the refusal implies that the reader is a poor credit risk, something none of us likes to be.

Refusal of Credit

Dear Mr. Murray:

1 Thank you for your promptness in sending us the credit information we

requested. I am glad to report that all your credit references spoke favorably of you as a businessman.

2   The new store which you are opening in Styptic should eventually prosper since yours is a thriving community. But its location within twenty miles of Megopolis forces you to compete with the larger stocks and lower prices of the metropolitan department stores, so readily accessible to commuters from Styptic. I feel that you can best meet such competition by starting with as little indebtedness as possible. Thus, at this point, we would like to do business with you on a cash basis only.

3   But I do have a suggestion. If you cut your order in half and pay cash for it, this will entitle you to our two percent cash discount, a saving which you can pass on to your customers. By ordering frequently in small quantities, you can best meet the competition through keeping up-to-date merchandise on your shelves. Thus, through cash buying you can establish your business on a sound basis that will entitle you to an excellent credit reputation.

4   The enclosed duplicate of your order will assist you in making your selection. Just check the items you wish and sign the order. Your merchandise will arrive C.O.D. within two days—in plenty of time for your opening sale.

Sincerely,

Can Mr. Murray be sure his request for credit received careful consideration?

_____

Yes (The writer uses specific words that only apply to Mr. Murray's problem. A letter like this cannot be written without the writer giving it some thought.)

7b   What about the reasons for the turndown? Are they in the letter? _____

Yes

7c   Although the reasons for the turndown are negative thoughts, are they stated unpleasantly? _____

No

7d   Where exactly is the actual refusal? _____

At the end of the second paragraph.

7e   Does the actual refusal come before or after the reasons for the refusal?

_____

after

7f   What has the writer done in the third paragraph? _____

He's supplied a positive alternative.

7g   Do you think the writer's company received Mr. Murray's reduced order?

_____

Yes (Of course they may not have, but more than likely they did.)

TAKE A LITTLE LONGER

8 Here's a general idea that sums up everything we have been saying about "no" letters:

If you can say yes, say it at once. If you must say no, take a little longer.

This suggests that "no" letters will often be longer than "yes" letters. Does this mean that you will have to pad them and violate the principle of conciseness?

No (Conciseness is saying what has to be said in the fewest possible words. If you're going to salvage the reader's goodwill, you will have to give him explanations, possible alternatives, and assurances of careful consideration. All these things *have* to be said.)

9 Let's quickly review the various techniques for writing "no" letters. The first and most important thing a writer can do in a turndown is _____ .

---

to explain the refusal, when possible.

10 An added touch which will often help to soften the blow of a refusal is an assurance of _____ .

---

careful consideration

11 You can best show your reader that you have carefully considered his request by _____ .

---

writing about details which apply to his situation and only his, being specific

12 Sometimes, when you are denying a specific request, you can often offer _____ .

(positive) alternatives

Now begin the exercises.

EXERCISES

Use your mask here.

A In this exercise, you have only two turndown letters to write. So don't rush headlong into the first sentence. Do some thinking and planning beforehand. Take your time.

Here's the first situation. You are a correspondent for a publishing company. You have received the first order from Spec's Book Store, Fresno, California 93707, for twenty sets of *Goffers' Encyclopedia*. You check with your credit agency which reports that this store is behind in its payments to its present suppliers. You decide not to give credit to Spec's.

There are several alternatives that you can offer: (1) Spec's can send cash, (2) Spec's can order C.O.D., or (3) Spec's can ask you to review their credit situation in three months.

Don't write off Spec's completely; you may be able to salvage something from this situation. It's a good idea to obtain their goodwill if you can.

Now begin to think of what you're going to put into your letter. What about the opening? You have to get a reason for the refusal and positive alternatives into the letter. In what order will they appear?

Now jot down your ideas. _____

We hope you didn't include ideas such as . . .

"Our credit agencies reported that you are behind in your payments to your present suppliers."

"We'd like to obtain your goodwill if we can."

We hope you have your ideas in the following order . . .

1 Opening sentence
2 Reason for refusal
3 Refusal (Omit, perhaps?)
4 Positive alternatives
5 Closing

Now write your first draft letter to Mr. Spec._____

Now go back over your letter and carefully polish it. Then check your letter with ours.

Refusal of Credit—2

Spec's Book Store
Fresno, California 93707

Gentlemen:

Tells what the letter is about
Thanks for sending your order for twenty sets of *Goffer's Encyclopedia*. I am glad to welcome you as a new customer.

Reason for refusal and refusal
Because our credit agencies report that the situation is not encouraging, I'm sorry that we cannot send you your order on account. **(Alternatives)** However, may we offer some alternatives? You can send cash or tell us to ship C.O.D. Or, if you wish, we will be happy to review your credit situation in three months.

Request for action
Please let me know what you decide to do.

Sincerely,

B Here's a tough problem: you are a correspondent for an insurance company. You have received a filled-in form from the Redstone Hospital. It shows that Mr.

James Garner, a medical policy owner, has applied for hospital benefits of $600. The company decides in his favor and sends him a check.

A few weeks later, during routine checking, you find that the Redstone is not an accredited hospital, and therefore Mr. Garner was not entitled to the benefits. Your boss decides to let it pass, but a note is made on Mr. Garner's file that the hospital is not accredited.

Six months later, Mr. Garner applies again. Once again, he has stayed at Redstone. You investigate, and find that the hospital is still not accredited. Since Mr. Garner's contract doesn't cover admissions to unaccredited hospitals, you now have to say no.

Remember that you approved his claim last time, but this time you're not going to. Mr. Garner may be much annoyed by your inconsistency. Furthermore, if Mr. Garner had known about the situation, he might have gone to a different hospital so that he could collect his benefits.

Now begin to marshal your reasons for your turndown. Think of the ideas for your opening sentence. At what point are you going to state the actual refusal? We hope you don't plan to put it in the beginning. And what ideas go into your closing sentence? Jot down your ideas, sort them, and then check below. _____

We hope that you didn't include such ideas as . . .

"You know that you were not entitled to the $600 that we paid last time."

"If you had gone to an accredited hospital, we would have been able to pay your claim."

We hope that you have stated your reasons before you state your refusal. We hope that you have included an apology for your error.

Using your jottings, write your first-draft letter. _____

Saying No to an Insurance Claim

Dear Mr. Garner:

Tells what letter is about and assures careful consideration
I have carefully considered your application for hospital benefits to pay for your recent stay at the Redstone Hospital.

Review of past transaction
I notice that you have received benefits for a previous stay there. When we received your first application, we assumed that the hospital was accredited and therefore we paid you the $600. Later we learned that the hospital was not accredited, but since we should have checked, we decided to let the situation stay as it was.

Reasons for refusal and refusal itself
Before writing you this time, I checked and found that the Redstone is still not accredited. Since your contract covers only admissions to accredited hos-

pitals, I hope that you will understand that we cannot pay your claim this time.

Apology for past mistake and courteous closing
I know this news will be a surprise to you, and I'm sorry that we must be so inconsistent. We'll try not to let it happen again.

Sincerely,

HELPFUL HINT

When you write a letter that says *no*, take a little longer and use the following techniques:

1 When possible, give reasons for the refusal—*before* the actual refusal.
2 Assure the reader of careful consideration by saying so and by using specific words.
3 Give positive alternatives whenever possible.
4 Be sure your tone is as friendly and positive as you can make it.

EIGHTEEN
PERSUADE YOUR READER

Higher education seeks to develop fully in students the ability to communicate effectively in writing. Writing that is clear, concise, and appropriate to the given reader is an asset in all walks of life, professional as well as personal. For example, if a person cannot communicate the results of his research, his work is sterile, no matter how imaginative or potentially useful it may be.

One's accomplishment is thus in a very real sense dependent upon the quality of his communication with others.

J. C. Warner, President Emeritus, Carnegie-Mellon University

In this final chapter, we are going to cover some of the techniques for persuading a reader to do something.

One type of letter whose success often depends on how well the writer has practiced the art of persuasion is the sales letter. Another is the collection letter. But the techniques of persuasion apply to almost all types of letters. Even a letter whose purpose is strictly goodwill is trying to nudge the reader in a certain direction.

SALES LETTERS

The purpose of a sales letter is obvious—to get the reader to *act*, either by taking some step which leads to a sale or by making the purchase itself. Most sales letters usually have the following parts:

1 An opening that gets the reader's *attention* or stimulates a *desire* for the writer's product or service
2 Evidence or reasoning that *convinces* the reader of the worthiness of the product or service
3 A call for *action*

Openings

One technique for capturing the reader's attention at the beginning of a sales letter is to appeal to his curiosity with a teaser, such as:

I have good news for you.

This is the one exception to our general rule that your opening sentence should tell the reader what your letter is about, because in this case you are trying to get a reaction, such as "What could the 'news' be?"

Another way to open a sales letter is to create a desire for the product or service. The emphasis is on the benefit—what the product or service will do *for* the reader, as in:

Would you be interested in learning to sew just like the professionals do—to make clothes for yourself and children, to create slipcovers, curtains, and other home furnishings—in short, to beat the high cost of living and have fun doing it?

Creating Conviction

There are as many ways to persuade someone of the worthiness of your product or service as there are sales pitches. They can range from a simple listing of its appealing or unique features to testimonials from superstars. But the main idea is to convince the reader that your product or service is the one that will best fulfill his desires.

Closings

The primary purpose of your closing sentence in a sales letter is to call for action—to tell the reader, clearly and specifically, what he is to *do*.

Use your mask here.

1a Below are some examples of the three ingredients of a *sales* letter. Which ones can get the reader's attention or create a desire for the writer's products or services? That is, which would make good openings? _____

    A. How would you like to cut your office overhead 40 percent without in any way sacrificing production?

    B. The *S.I.C. Directory* gives you up-to-date, accurate information on every phase of motor-freight shipping—how to do it, whom to contact, the best routes, etc.

    C. Wouldn't you be interested in a larger share of good health than you've been enjoying lately?

    D. Fill in the enclosed card right now and return it with your check or money order for $7.20 (no cash, please), and we'll begin mailing you the *Investor's Bulletin* every week for a full year.

    E. Our representative will be making house-to-house calls in your neighborhood in the next few days. Look for him.

    F. Prepton motor oil is made expressly for modern engines which, due to high power output and compression, require a lubricating oil that can withstand extreme working temperatures and pressures.

    G. You're in Chamonix, France, climbing slowly in a cable car up the side of snow-capped Mont Blanc, the highest mountain in the Alps. As the Petit Jardin, where you just enjoyed a delicious gourmet lunch, dwindles below, one of the most magnificent panoramas in the world unfolds about you.

    A, C, G

1b The remaining examples above are either those that are designed to convince the reader or to close a sales letter. Which ones are designed to convince the reader of the worthiness of the product or service being sold? _____

    B and F (D and E are closings.)

Sales Letter

2a You're the public relations consultant for the Green Mountain Inn, a year-round resort complex in Weston, Vermont. You're sitting down in late April to write a sales letter that will be sent to a mailing list of middle- to upper-income families in the urban and suburban communities of the Northeast.

    The Inn consists of a six-hundred-room main hotel and fifty cottages, all set on seven thousand acres of the scenic Green Mountains and overlooking Elfin Lake. Cottages range in size from two to six rooms. In the winter, there's skiing, tobogganning, and ice skating—while in the summer, there's boating, swimming, golf at the famous eighteen-hole Burning Branch course, riding, tennis, and walking or hiking on the many trails through the surrounding forests.

    Two restaurants—the Ethan Allen Coffee Shoppe and the White Stag—feature good, hearty New England cooking. There's also the Boar's Head Cocktail Lounge and the Meeting Room, where movies and variety entertainment are presented every night, with dancing every Friday and Saturday night.

The resort is only four hours from New York City on the thruway (Route 84) and two hours from Boston. Also, it is near the charming village of Woodstock with its summer theater, art shows, concerts, historic museums, country store, and craft shops.

An analysis of the Inn's past clientele indicates that 60 percent were families, 20 percent were honeymooners, 15 percent were young singles (who came primarily for the skiing), and 5 percent were miscellaneous.

The Inn has always prided itself on its informal, friendly atmosphere and has sought customers who could afford the prices and who were congenial to other guests. There is no pressure to join in "social activities" because the emphasis is on relaxation and peace.

This year management is trying to increase the average stay of its guests by offering a 10 percent discount for each day that a guest stays over seven days. Thus, if a guest stays for ten days, he gets the discount for three of those days.

There will be two enclosures with your letter: (1) a brochure giving the exact rates for the summer season (June 6 to September 6) and describing in words and pictures all the features and attractions of the Inn, and (2) a self-addressed, stamped postcard for the reader to fill in and return in order to make reservations. (Reservations can also be made by calling collect to (802) 824-3493.)

Now let's see what kind of sales letter you can write. First, think about what will go in your opening sentence. Remember, most of the people who will open your letter will know nothing of the Green Mountain Inn—so you want to get their interest or create a desire for your "product" right away. Which of the following would be the *best* opening for your letter? _____

A.   It's springtime again—time to start making plans for the summer.

B.   Are you out of ideas about what to do on your vacation this summer?

C.   What's your bag? Is it swimming, sailing, golf? Is it clean mountain air and some of the most beautiful scenery in the country? Is it dancing into the wee hours with your favorite chick? Well, all this and more can be yours at the Green Mountain Inn this coming summer.

D.   Swimming . . . hiking . . . golf . . . some of the most beautiful scenery in the country . . . hearty New England cooking . . . good times in a relaxed, peaceful atmosphere—enjoy all this and more by vacationing this coming summer at the Green Mountain Inn.

E.   Did you spend your summer vacation last year stuck in the fumes of traffic or looking frantically at the last minute for a motel near some noisy highway? Then perhaps you should spend this coming summer at our place—the Green Mountain Inn.

We like D the best. (A is all right, but we feel it is too mild and vague to really capture attention. The reader's reaction to B might be "no," and then he might throw the letter away. C has too much slang for most of the people who will read this letter. E might be effective for those who did not enjoy their vacation last summer, but only for them. We think D is the best because it quickly gives the reader a specific idea of what it would be like to enjoy the "product." It is more likely to create desire.

2b The next task is to *convince* the reader that your hotel can best fulfill his desires. You can do this by explaining, concisely, the attractions and advantages that the Inn has to offer. Remember that the brochure does this in detail, so select what you think are the most telling points. Also, be sure to include mention of the discount. First, jot down the ideas you will include in this section of the letter. Do not write complete sentences yet and do not include ideas for the closing. _____

Please resist the temptation to look at our answer before you write your own. That way you will obtain the most benefit from the lesson.

Here is our list of attractions:

1 Extensiveness and variety of lodging facilities—for both families and honeymooners.
2 Mention of Elfin Lake set in 7,000 acres of beautiful Green Mountain.
3 Description of summer sports facilities—with special mention of the golf course.
4 Hearty New England cooking served in the two restaurants.
5 Cocktail lounge, dancing, and entertainment in Meeting Room.
6 Attractions of nearby Woodstock.
7 Explanation of discount.
8 Summary of attractions with appeal to spend vacation at the Inn.

2c Now list those ideas that will go into the closing of this sales letter. _____

Here is our list:

1 Talk the idea over with family or friends.
2 Fill in postcard for reservations.
3 Or call (802) 824-3493.
4 You will receive immediate and interested attention.

2d Now write the second two parts of this sales letter. _____

Again, please do not peek at our answer before writing your own.

Dear _____ :

Creates desire
Swimming . . . hiking . . . golf . . . some of the most beautiful scenery in the country . . . hearty New England cooking . . . good times in a relaxed peaceful atmosphere—enjoy all this and more, by vacationing this coming summer at the Green Mountain Inn.

Extensiveness and variety of lodgings, and description of setting
It makes no difference if you're on your honeymoon or bringing a family of twelve. You'll find the kind of vacation lodging that's just right for you—at either our six-hundred-room hotel *or* in one of our fifty private cottages. All this overlooks our own Elfin Lake, set amid 7,000 acres of the unspoiled, historic Green Mountains of Vermont.

Description of sports and recreational facilities
As you can see from the enclosed brochure, we have all sorts of summer sports and recreational facilities—for all ages. This year our eighteen-hole Burning Branch golf course, one of the better known courses in America, is in exceptionally good condition and greens fees are quite reasonable.

Dining entertainment
But no matter what your sporting preferences, you're sure to enjoy the hospitality of our Boar's Head Cocktail Lounge and the fine New England cooking served in our two modern restaurants—the Ethan Allen Coffee Shoppe and the White Stag. Evenings, there's movies and variety entertainment in the Meeting Room—with dancing every Friday and Saturday night. And in the nearby village of Woodstock you'll find summer theater, art shows, concerts, historic museums, a country store, and craft shops.

Discount
This year, we're offering a special discount to those guests who stay with us for more than seven days. You get 10 percent off the summer rates—as listed in the brochure—for each day past the first seven. Thus, if you stay ten days, you get 10 percent off for the last three.

Summary of attractions
So if it's healthy, relaxed times you want—in beautiful surroundings—with congenial people of like mind, come stay with us this summer. Talk it over with your family and friends. (**Request for action**) Just fill in and mail the enclosed postcard, or call us collect at (802) 824-3493. Your reservation or request for information will receive our immediate and interested attention.

Sincerely yours,

COLLECTION LETTERS

3a   Like the sales letter, the collection letter is written to persuade the reader—in this case, to pay an overdue bill. Usually, a collection letter has the following elements:

1   An *opening* that states the business at hand—the amount due, dates of previous correspondence, order numbers, etc.
2   A line of *reasoning* to convince the reader to pay or at least take some affirmative action
3   A specific request for *action*

Below are some examples of the three elements of collection letters. Which ones are designed to *open* such letters? _____

A. This is just a friendly reminder that our bill to you of January 8 for $304.71 is still outstanding.

B. We appreciate your business—we don't want to annoy you—and yet we expect you to live up to our terms of 3 percent ten days, thirty days net, since we must meet our own obligations too.

C. I have been wondering if perhaps there is something more we can do to complete your order for automotive parts for $1,286.94, which we shipped to you on June 8, because we have not yet received payment.

D. Please send your check to us by April 2—to cover your November statement.

E. If you will enclose your check for $962.87 with your new order for office supplies, we will be happy to ship them to you right away.

F. I'm sure, Mr. Oberon, that you prize your good credit rating. Won't you retain yours and at the same time be able to take advantage of our special discount offer, as described in the enclosed brochure?

G. If you are not able to send us a check right now, may we at least hear from you soon? Perhaps we can work something out.

H. Perhaps you have overlooked paying us the amount due since it is so small, but I'm sure you would like to have your account with us as neat and tidy as possible.

A and C

3b The remaining examples above demonstrate either lines of reasoning to convince the reader to pay or closings. Which are the closings? _____

D, E, and G

Collection Letter

4a In writing a collection letter, keep in mind that 95 percent of all the people who use credit pay their bills on time, 4 percent are slow payers, and only 1 percent never pay. Thus, most of the collection letters you will ever write are to people who will eventually pay. So it is extremely important that you not only persuade the reader to pay but keep his goodwill and perhaps obtain new business from him as well. Your tone should be firm but never angry, contemptuous, or pitying. Try to be fair and understanding but never apologize for requesting payment. Above all don't threaten, unless absolutely necessary. Only as a last resort is a threat used such as, "If we do not receive payment within ten days, we will put the matter in the hands of our attorneys."

With all this in mind, let's get down to writing a collection letter. Here's the situation.

You are the credit manager of Peabody-Morrison, Inc., a large book distributor. The selling terms of your firm are 5 percent—thirty days, net—sixty days. This means that if a customer pays a bill within thirty days from the billing date, he benefits from a **5** percent discount and that he is expected to pay the bill in full within sixty days.

Your computer sent a bill for $10,647.10 to Arthur T. Penn, proprietor of Penn's Bookshop. He has just returned your bill without payment but with the handwritten comment, "I knew inflation was here, but I didn't think it was this bad." Actually, Mr. Penn is thirty days past due on his account for $647.10. He has been a customer for about a year, with orders averaging about $250 per month. This is the first time that he has been late in making payment.

Your job is to write an appropriate collection letter. Do you think it would be a good idea to avoid mention of the computer's error?_____

No (We're all human. When you apologize for your error, you build goodwill.)

4b   Do you think it would be a good idea to remind Mr. Penn that his account is now past due? _____

Yes

4c   Which of the following adjectives best describes the tone that your letter should take? _____

A.   Friendly but firm.
B.   Apologetic about asking for the payment.
C.   Insistent.

A (We think that at this point in your dealings with Mr. Penn you should give him the benefit of the doubt. Thus, you should be friendly but not hesitant about asking for what is due.)

4d   Now jot down the ideas you will include in your letter. Do not write full sentences yet. _____

Here are our jottings:

1   Sorry about error.
2   Correct amount: $647.10.
3   Account now past due.
4   Request for prompt payment.

4e   Now write your letter to Mr. Penn. _____

Dear Mr. Penn:

Tells what the letter is about
I'm not quite sure what strange technical quirk made our computer add ten thousand dollars to your last bill from us. (**Apology for computer error**) In any event, please accept my apologies.
The correct amount of this bill is $647.10.

Reminder and request for payment
I notice that your account is now somewhat past due, so may I have your check for the correct amount as soon as possible? Thank you.

Sincerely yours,

4f Another thirty days goes by, and you hear nothing from Mr. Penn. His account is now sixty days past due; that is, four months have passed since the original billing date. Moreover, you have received no new orders from him.

You are sitting down to write your second—and, you hope, your last—collection letter to Mr. Penn. Which of the following do you think you should do in your letter? You may want to do more than one. _____

- A. Give Mr. Penn a short, friendly reminder that payment is overdue. (This assumes that he has simply forgotten to pay.)
- B. Ask for an explanation of the delay and offer the possibility of "working something out." (This assumes that there are good reasons for the non-payment.)
- C. Remind him of the importance of maintaining a sound credit rating.
- D. Ask for payment.
- E. Threaten legal action.
- F. Tell him of new list of the latest books and offer to fill new order—as soon as payment comes.

B, possibly C, D, and possibly F (We would not choose A because too much water has gone under the bridge to assume Mr. Penn has simply forgotten to pay. And we would not choose E, because there may very well be a good reason why Mr. Penn did not answer your last letter. For example, he may have been on vacation, or he may be experiencing temporary financial difficulties. Thus, we feel that B is a good choice and perhaps C. D, of course, is always done in a collection letter. F might also be a good idea, particularly if you assume that your letter will be effective.)

4g Now jot down the ideas that will go in your letter. Do not write complete sentences yet. _____

1 Account for $647.10 seriously past due.
2 Ask for explanation of delay—with offer of help.
3 Sell him on importance of a good credit rating.
4 We have a new list of the latest books and will welcome new orders—as soon as payment comes.
5 Request for payment.

4h Now write your letter. _____

To get full benefit, don't look at our answer before composing your own.

Dear Mr. Penn:

Tells what letter is about
Your account with us for $647.10 is now seriously past due. Perhaps there is a good reason. (**Request for explanation**) So, if you cannot send your check as payment in full, we would like to at least hear from you with an explanation. Perhaps we can work something out.

Appeal to reader's self interest
By doing so, you will be taking a major step toward preserving your good credit rating, which is lifeblood to most businesses.

Offer of new goods
We have just published our new list of the latest books, which I am sure you will want to place on your shelves. We would welcome new orders from you and will ship them out as soon as your account is up to date.

Request for action
May we hear from you right away?

Sincerely,

ONE FINAL WORD

In this course you have learned the principles and techniques for making your letters effective. But now you must really begin to work. For only a continued, sustained application of them will give you ease and skill in writing.

The task of acquiring and improving new skills is always hard, but it is particularly hard in writing. Because writing is such a personal process, it is difficult for the writer to admit that his is only passable and that it could be much better.

Nevertheless, professional writers are always conscious of their skills and always try to improve. Carl Sandburg stated this position when, seventy-two years old and world-famous, he said:

"I am still studying verbs and the mystery of how they connect nouns. I am more suspicious of adjectives than at any other time in all my born days . . . All my life I have been trying to learn to read, to see and hear, and to write . . . It could be, in the grace of God, I shall live to be eighty-nine, as did Hokusai, and speaking my farewell to earthly scenes, I might paraphrase: 'If God had let me live five years longer I should have been a writer. "

If you are paid to write in business, you are a professional writer and thus will want to be a craftsman at your trade. Yet how many people who earn their living by writing in business can meet the basic requirements of a professional? Obviously a pianist should be able to answer questions like: "Can you find middle C?" "Can you run a scale?" It should be equally obvious (but is not) that a business writer should be able to answer questions like: "Can you deflate this sentence?" "Can you find the main verb of your sentence?" "Can you change a passive sentence to an active one?"

As apprentices, we acquire our basic principles and techniques. After much practice and study, we become master craftsmen—effective letter writers.

Now turn to the final exercises.

EXERCISES

Persuasive Letter

A Study the following situation carefully: you are the Tax Collector of Greenbriar County, a large suburban community, with a population of almost one million. You are sitting down to write a letter, a copy of which will be mailed along with each property-tax bill to each property owner in the county. The purpose of your letter is to convince the taxpayer *not* to request a receipt for his property-tax payment.

Past procedure has been for the taxpayer to return the entire bill with his payment and within four to six weeks, your office would return the receipted bill to him. But now a receipt will not be issued unless the taxpayer specifically asks for it. For one thing, the bill itself has been redesigned. The bill now has a left side containing the taxpayer's name and address, a description of the property being taxed, the amount of tax, and other pertinent information. There is even a space for the taxpayer to note the date and number of the check he uses in making payment. The idea is for the taxpayer to keep the left side and return the right-hand stub with his payment. With this new system, there will be no waiting period during which the taxpayer may not have the necessary information concerning his tax payment.

When your office receives the right-hand stub and the taxpayer's payment, an identifying number is printed on both, so that they can be located at any time. This will improve the accuracy and accountability of your tax-collection system—two qualities which are so important to keeping the public trust.

The courts have ruled that a canceled check is a more conclusive proof of payment than a tax bill receipted by the Tax Collector. The reason **for** this is that some checks are returned to the Tax Collector unpaid, and your office is then forced to void the payment on its records. However, the taxpayer may already have a receipted bill. Moreover, the Internal Revenue Service agrees that a canceled check is sufficient proof of payment when claiming deductions on federal income-tax returns.

Your accountants estimate that your office can effect a savings of about $20,000 in operating costs if staff time is not taken up with the job of receipting property-tax payments.

Taxpayers can make special requests for receipts by calling Mrs. Klingeman at 417-8308 or writing her at your office.

Now analyze the information we have given you. First, think about your opening. There are several benefits to the new system which the reader may be interested in. Which will most appeal to him? Now think of the body of your letter. Which reasons for not requesting tax receipts are most powerful? Remember, we have given you a lot of information, so you want to select only that which will best suit your purpose—without making your letter too long. All right, now think of your closing. You want to make a specific appeal for action (or, in this case, nonaction).

Now jot down the ideas you will include in your letter. Do not write complete sentences yet. _____

Use your mask here.

Here is our list of ideas:

1 You can help save the county $20,000.
2 Don't ask for receipts.
3 No tax receipts unless you ask.
4 Canceled check is more conclusive proof—say the courts.
5 IRS agrees.
6 An added benefit: keeping left-hand portion of bill ensures having necessary information at all times.
7 If you still want receipt, call or write Klingeman.
8 Please don't ask, unless absolutely necessary.

Now write your letter. _____

Dear_____:

Gets interest with description of benefit
Would you be interested in helping us save Briarcliff County an estimated $20,000 in operating costs? You can do so by *not* requesting receipts for your property-tax payments.

More reasons for the request not to ask for receipts
This year you will not receive a receipt unless you ask for one. Aside from the savings to the county, there are several reasons why this change has been made. First, the courts have ruled that your canceled check is more conclusive proof of payment than a receipted bill from the Tax Collector. (Some checks are returned to us unpaid, and we have to void the payment on our records. However, the taxpayer may already have a receipted bill.) Second, the Internal Revenue Service agrees that a canceled check is sufficient proof of payment when claiming deductions on federal income-tax returns.

Another benefit of the new procedure
There's another benefit from the changes we've made in your tax bill itself. Previously, you had to return the whole bill with your payment, and we then sent you the receipted bill within four to six weeks—thus leaving a period when you probably had no specific records of the transaction. Now, you can simply keep the left portion of your bill, which has all the pertinent information, and mail us the right-hand stub with your payment. There's even a space on the left side for you to note the date and number of your check.

Renewed request for restraint and repetition of most telling reason for it
If you have any questions or you want a receipt, write Mrs. Klingeman at this office, or call her at 417-8308. But please, ask for receipts only if you have an exceptionally good reason. Your canceled check is your best proof of payment.

                                        Sincerely,

Letter of Application

B Here's the situation. You are soon to graduate from college and have missed an appointment you made with Alfred T. Malkin, Vice President and recruiter from the California National Bank, because you were ill the entire week he was on campus. Because the Home Office of the bank is in San Francisco (P.O. Box 1148, zip code 94129) more than a thousand miles away, you must now apply by mail and hope that your letter will be persuasive enough so that he will offer to pay your way out for a personal interview.

Having missed the interview, you don't know whether there are any specific openings for you at the bank, but you have read its annual report and know several things about the organization:

1　It is the largest commercial bank in the U.S., with assets of more than $30 billion, almost 1,000 branches in California and another 100 overseas.
2　It is currently involved, as are many organizations, in a special interest of yours; a social-action program involving ecology, consumerism, and minority programs.
3　According to the annual report, there is a management training program, consisting of both work and study, that prepares college graduates for careers in either lending or operations and encourages them to choose the field they feel best suited for.

Your father is a bank officer in the Town Bank of EauClaire, Wisconsin. You have worked for his bank as a teller and operations assistant during the last three summer vacations from college. You enjoy the banking atmosphere.

When writing your letter, remember that recruiters look for certain qualities in job applicants. These are revealed mostly during personal interviews but also in applicants' letters and résumés (data sheets). These qualities include good appearance, conversational ability, likeableness, mental alertness, poise and maturity, aggressiveness, judgment, and enthusiasm. At the same time, recruiters seek applicants who are *special*—who have the spark of creativity and individuality, flexibility, maturity beyond their years, and perhaps a deeper-than-usual understanding of the business they hope to work for.

Your job is to persuade the recruiter that you *are* special. Your letter must stand out from the many he will receive that day. Remember that you're writing a sales letter—you're selling yourself. You must get the recruiter's attention, convince him of your worthiness, and get the action you want. To do this, put yourself in the situation we have described above, but when you are describing grades, skills, social activities, etc., use details from your own background. Now jot down the ideas you want to include in the beginning, middle, and close of your application letter. You do not have to write complete sentences yet. _____

Here is our list of ideas:

1　Refer to the cancelation of the interview.
2　I especially wanted to see you because of my interest in banking. (I'm special and I understand banking.)
3　My background and interests.
4　Request for action.

Now write your letter of application, using details from your own experience where appropriate. Mention all *your* good points. Be sure to include everything that will get attention, convince the reader of your value, and get the action you want.

Mr. Alfred T. Malkin
Vice President
California National Bank
San Francisco, California 94129

Dear Mr. Malkin:

Tells what the letter is about and captures interest by stating career interest
Because banking is my first choice of careers, I particularly wanted to meet you last week on your visit to our campus. But I was ill the entire week and still had a fever when I called to cancel the appointment.

Gives strong point: I already know banking
In any case, may I tell you about myself? My father has been an official of the Town Bank in EauClaire, Wisconsin, for many years, and I have worked in the bank as a teller and operations assistant during my last three summer vacations from college. When I was younger, I ran errands for bank officers. So while I'm far from being an expert, I do understand the basics of banking and find the profession both important and congenial.

My education, social activities, and interests
During my studies for the BBA degree at college, I have continued my education in banking-related subjects and have maintained high grades (a 3.4 out of a possible 4.0), while participating in social activities. My membership in Alpha Kappa Psi business professional fraternity has provided a stimulating social environment on campus. This has been balanced by my membership in Big Brothers and in the Police Athletic League.

I'm as community-minded as you are
The opportunity for an association with the California Bank is particularly exciting, not because of your size alone but because of the bank's present and potential influence on business and society. This is a complex subject, I know, that requires the establishment of appropriate priorities. But I imagine the bank will always want to stimulate community activities by individual employees, whose day-to-day activities will also help determine just what our quality of life is going to be.

I've done my homework on your bank
Although I'm not certain whether lending or operations work would be more congenial in the long run, I appreciate the option presented by your management training program to turn in either direction.

May I talk with you further about my qualifications? I would be happy to come to San Francisco at any time convenient to you.

Sincerely,

HELPFUL HINT

When you are faced with writing a letter in which you must persuade the reader, ask yourself the following questions:

1 In my *opening*, did I capture the reader's attention or create desire for my product or service?
2 In the *body*, did I present a line of reasoning that is clear, convincing, and appropriate?
3 In my *closing*, did I make my request for action so clear that the reader will have no doubt about what he is supposed to do?

If your answer to these questions is yes, you probably have written a persuasive letter.

"I wanted to make one thing crystal clear
but I forgot what it was."

APPENDIX
MECHANICS OF BUSINESS LETTERS

The famous letter-writer Lord Chesterfield has said of writing that

"Style is the dress of thoughts."

He's right. The *way* you present a message is inseparable from what you say. For no matter how well you have written your letter, the manner in which it is presented can determine whether it is effective or not. Thus, the appearance of your letters can enhance or undermine their effectiveness. As your own experience will testify, appearance creates an immediate impression that, if favorable, can nudge the reader in the direction you want him to go, or, if unfavorable, can bring a negative reaction immediately.

LETTER LAYOUT

Although authorities agree that there is no "correct" letter-writing layout, three basic forms are generally recognized:

1 *Semiblock form*, the most common one, is a middle-of-the-road layout used by New York Life Insurance Company for all its correspondence. It is easy to type and has a modern appearance that does not call attention to itself.
2 *Block form* is the most modern and is the quickest and easiest to type.
3 *Modified block form* combines some of the features of both semiblock and block form.

Following are examples of the three letter-layout forms.

Semiblock Form

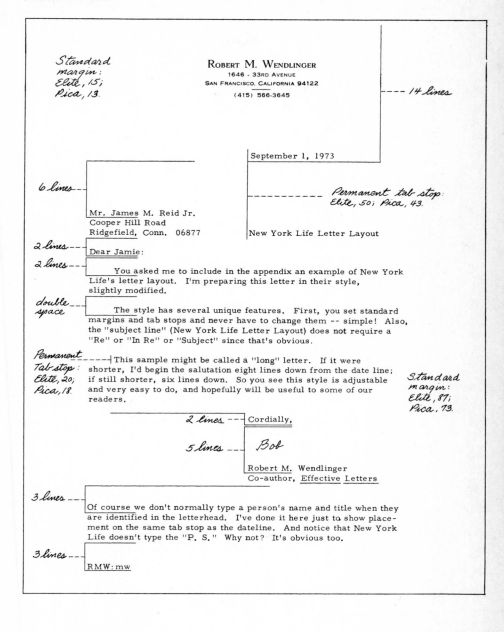

Standard margin: Elite, 15; Pica, 13.

ROBERT M. WENDLINGER
1646 - 33RD AVENUE
SAN FRANCISCO, CALIFORNIA 94122
(415) 566-3645

---- 14 lines

September 1, 1973

6 lines --

---------- Permanent tab stop: Elite, 50; Pica, 43.

Mr. James M. Reid Jr.
Cooper Hill Road
Ridgefield, Conn. 06877

New York Life Letter Layout

2 lines --- Dear Jamie:

2 lines ---
You asked me to include in the appendix an example of New York
Life's letter layout. I'm preparing this letter in their style,
slightly modified.

double space ---
The style has several unique features. First, you set standard
margins and tab stops and never have to change them -- simple! Also,
the "subject line" (New York Life Letter Layout) does not require a
"Re" or "In Re" or "Subject" since that's obvious.

Permanent Tab stop: Elite, 20; Pica, 18.
This sample might be called a "long" letter. If it were
shorter, I'd begin the salutation eight lines down from the date line;
if still shorter, six lines down. So you see this style is adjustable
and very easy to do, and hopefully will be useful to some of our
readers.

Standard margin: Elite, 87; Pica, 73.

2 lines --- Cordially,

5 lines --- Bob

Robert M. Wendlinger
Co-author, Effective Letters

3 lines ---
Of course we don't normally type a person's name and title when they
are identified in the letterhead. I've done it here just to show placement on the same tab stop as the dateline. And notice that New York
Life doesn't type the "P. S." Why not? It's obvious too.

3 lines ---
RMW:mw

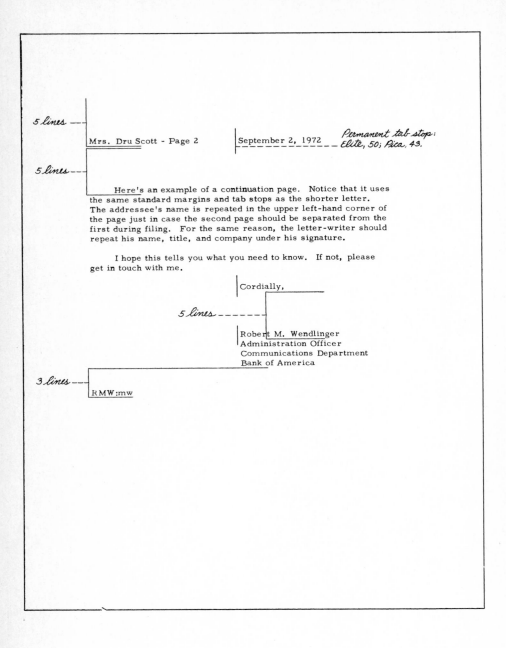

5 lines ——

Mrs. Dru Scott - Page 2 | September 2, 1972 *Permanent tab stop: Elite, 50; Pica, 43.*

5 lines ——

Here's an example of a continuation page. Notice that it uses the same standard margins and tab stops as the shorter letter. The addressee's name is repeated in the upper left-hand corner of the page just in case the second page should be separated from the first during filing. For the same reason, the letter-writer should repeat his name, title, and company under his signature.

I hope this tells you what you need to know. If not, please get in touch with me.

Cordially,

5 lines ——

Robert M. Wendlinger
Administration Officer
Communications Department
Bank of America

3 lines ——

RMW:mw

Block Form

> James M. Reid Company
> Cooper Hill Road
> Ridgefield, Connecticut 06877
>
> September 8, 1973
>
> Mr. Robert M. Wendlinger
> 1646-33rd Avenue
> San Francisco, California 94122
>
> Dear Bob:
>
> As you asked, I'm writing you in the most modern of the letter layouts—the block form. It is still fairly rare in business but is gaining in popularity because it is easy and fast for the typist.
>
> As you can see, everything is flush left on the margin. Notice that the letter is single-spaced, even though it is quite short—with double-spaces between paragraphs.
>
> Sincerely,
>
> *James M. Reid*
>
> James M. Reid
> Co-author, *Effective Letters*
>
> JMR:lh

Modified Block Form

James M. Reid
Cooper Hill Road
Ridgefield, Connecticut 06877
September 8, 1973

Mr. Robert M. Wendlinger
1646-33rd Avenue
San Francisco, California 94122

Dear Bob:

This modified block form is quite popular among students and others who are writing business letters on stationery not having a letterhead. It is also widely used by organizations that *do* have a letterhead centered at the top.

Notice that it is exactly the same as the block style except that the date, complimentary close, signature, typed signature, and title are on the right, as in the semiblock form.

Best,

James M. Reid
Co-author, *Effective Letters*

JMR:lh

PARTS OF THE LETTER

The Heading

The heading consists of the writer's complete address and the date. It always includes the zip code and sometimes the name and title of the writer. For example:

Regent Industries, Inc.
1120 Applegate Road
Briarcliff Manor, New York 10510

Arthur T. Burns, President

September 8, 1973

Field and Walinski
Attorneys-at-Law

Max R. Field	7-9 Isaac Street	Telephone
George L. Walinski	Norwalk, Connecticut 06852	853-3009
Jules Lang		Area Code 203
Melvin S. Silverman		

September 8, 1973

Note the form of the date above. It is the only correct form. The following are not:

INCORRECT: Sept. 8, 1973
                      9/8/73
                      September 8th, 1973

In the body of the letter, it's correct to add *th*, or *st, d, rd* after the day of the month, as in, "on the 8th of September," "on the eighth of September," or "on the 8th."

The Inside Address

This is the reader's address and should be exactly the same as his address on the envelope.

If the reader is a man, write "Mr." or his personal title and his official title below. For example:

Mr. Thorsten F. Krone
Vice President—Operations

Dr. Wilbur F. Conners
Chairman of the Board

If the reader is a woman, write "Miss," "Mrs.," "Ms.," or her personal title:

Miss Alice P. Raymond
Special Assistant

Mrs. Helen G. Turner
Treasurer

Dr. Linn Harding
Chief of Orthopedics

Write out the names of titles, streets, and states. Be sure to include the zip code.

CORRECT	INCORRECT
Mr. Robert Jud	Mr. Robt. Jud
Vice President	VP
Marsh and McKennon, Inc.	Marsh and McKennon
1121 Seventh Avenue	1121 7th Ave.
New York, New York 10017	New York, N.Y.

The Salutation

The salutation in a business letter is *always* followed by a colon, even if you address the reader by his first name. Below are the most common salutations:

Dear Mr. Wilkes:	Gentlemen:
Dear Miss Galloway:	Ladies:
Dear Dr. Hartman:	Dear Sir:
Dear Don:	Dear Sirs:

Always use your reader's name in the salutation, if you know it. When you do not have a specific name to write to, write "Gentlemen" or "Dear Sirs"—unless the organization is all female.

The Subject Line

Although the subject line should usually be avoided, some organizations want it included to tell the reader quickly what the letter is referring to. It is particularly appropriate when you are writing in reference to something that has a number. In semiblock style, the subject line is placed to the right of the last line of the inside address (see page 239). In block and modified block style, it goes between the inside address and the salutation. For example:

September 8, 1973

Recon Distributors, Inc.
118 West Olive Street
Macon, Georgia 31207

Invoice #186846

Gentlemen:

The word "Subject:" is still sometimes used ("Subject: Cost Estimates for Contract 178-A"), but today's trend is to omit it. Do not use "Re" or "In re." They are archaic.

The Complimentary Close

If your letter is to a stranger, the following closes are appropriate:

Yours truly,
Yours very truly,

If you are writing to someone you know quite well, the following closes are more friendly:

Sincerely yours,   Cordially yours,

Sincerely,   Best,

Do not use stilted or cute closings, such as:

Yours in haste,   Yours till the cows come home,

Very faithfully yours,   Your obedient servant,

And do not attach such phrases as "I remain . . ." or "We are . . ." to the end of the body of your letter.

The Signature

Your signature may take various forms, depending on your organization's policy and what is in your letterhead.

If your name and title are in the letterhead, then only your signature is sufficient, as in:

Sincerely yours,

Chester

If your name and title are not in the letterhead, the following is correct:

Sincerely yours,

Ronald F. Porter

Ronald F. Porter
Office Manager

Some organizations want to have their names in the signature also, as in:

Sincerely yours,   Sincerely yours,

THE GREEN COMPANY

Ronald F. Porter   *Ronald F. Porter*

Ronald F. Porter   Ronald F. Porter
Office Manager   Office Manager
                               THE GREEN COMPANY

It's good practice for women to indicate, under their signature, how they wish to be addressed.

Jane D. Fowler   *Felicity N. Gates*

(Miss) Jane D. Fowler   Felicity N. Gates
                               (Mrs. John T. Gates)

Initials

The initials of the writer and typist are usually placed flush with the left margin, slightly below the signature. The writer's initials precede the colon; the typist's follow it. For example:

JMR:lh   JMR:LH   jmr:lh

Enclosures

Enclosures are indicated by writing the word "Enclosures" or the abbreviations "Encl." or "Enc." below the initials. If there is more than one enclosure, add the number. Examples:

Enclosures 2   Encl. 4

Copies

If copies (*cc* is the abbreviation) of the letter are to be sent to others besides the reader, include an entry such as the following:

JMR:lh   JMR:lh

Enc. 3   Enc. 3

Copies to: Mrs. Patricia Marlow   cc: Mr. A. Pomeroy
            Commander F. Wright Davis   Miss Williams

QUIZZES

CHAPTER 1

The following ten sentences have examples of incorrect, unnecessary, and wordy usages. Correct them.

1   In the normal course of procedure, we try to write all our clients with regard to their investments, irregardless of the amount invested.

2   I wish to tell you that we have found a replacement for Mr. Johnson during the time of his stay in the hospital.

3   Miss Halvorsen has suggested a very unique approach to our financial problem; so its important that she receive her bonus at an early date.

4   Because of the fact that the Elktown plant is already operating at peak capacity, we must give some thought and consideration to the above stated alternative.

5   I personally feel that too many customers are returning back to the shop in order to complain about the service.

6   The plant manager was literally stampeded into a hasty decision.

7   I would like to answer in the affirmative, but I feel the action you suggest would have an adverse affect on sales. This fact has been overlooked by your planners.

8   Soon after the X-38 washing machines first began to sell well, we made a full and complete study along the lines of projected sales.

9   We have, at the present time, a complete line of women's fashions, which I will be glad to show to Mr. Fellini on the occasion of his arrival at our New York office.

10   All of the drawings, plans, photos, and etc. will arrive at your warehouse on or before June 12.

CHAPTER 2

Revise the following ten sentences so that they have no words or phrases that are incorrect, unnecessary, wordy, archaic, inflated, or confusingly technical.

1   As per the conditions of our contract, you will herewith find our check in the amount of $2,700.

2   In the event that you cannot get a mortgage on or before the end of the month, I deem it advisable for you to think about buying a less expensive home.

3   The mechanic advised me that the Ford had a large dent in it's right-rear fender, prior to the accident.

4   I regret to inform you that we have not been able to reach Mr. Clayton in re his overdue account.

5   We are in receipt of the same identical information that you have.

6   Your letter with reference to your clock radio has been duly noted with gratitude.

7   Pursuant to your request, I am sending you a list of all shipments sent subsequent to June 10.

8   We have initiated a series of three-day seminars on the basic fundamentals of selling bank services, but this series is the only one we are at the present time offering.

9 Although the boxes were small in size, they were very heavy and had to be handled in accordance with local regulations.
10 In view of the fact that the panel has decided to act along the lines that Mrs. Podesta suggested, I personally feel that we owe her an apology.

CHAPTER 3

Being verbs and general action verbs make the following ten sentences inconcise and weak. Make them shorter and more forceful by using specific action verbs.

1 It is my understanding that . . .
2 If there is an increase in prices by us, there is a chance of our endangering our competitive edge.
3 Mr. W. Endlinger's recommendation was that an audit of Red Stone, Inc.'s records be done by a C.P.A.
4 The use of punched cards results in a reduction of the time for processing credit transactions.
5 A check of all the charges on your furnace repair bill was made by Miss Cates.
6 John Williams is a person who can be of great help to your organization.
7 Completion of the project by you should be accomplished by October 28.
8 Because our shipping department is undergoing a reorganization, a delay in shipping your order has arisen.
9 The comptroller has effected a complete overhaul of the company's accounting procedures.
10 There was an overloading of the circuits by the new transformer.

CHAPTER 4

The following ten sentences contain passive and linking constructions. Revise them so that *every* subject-verb combination becomes *active*.

1 After your payment is recorded by the Home Office, a receipt is then mailed to you by them.
2 We have been informed by the credit bureau of your change of address.
3 Information was obtained from a variety of sources by the research team.
4 The high freshman-dropout rate may be caused by the fact that there was faulty high school preparation.
5 Our survey was cut short because of a lack of time.
6 The best photographs were separated from the other contest entries by the staff and were placed in a large red box.
7 Sending a preliminary report through normal channels was Mr. Finney's plan.
8 A test of the ore will be made by our chemists to determine its uranium content.
9 Achievement of a production rate of two thousand units per hour was the desire of the men in Section C.
10 This manual was written by Mr. Masters for brokers who are of service to the public

CHAPTER 5

Complete each sentence below by choosing the most *specific* word or phrase.

1 We wished to obtain further information, so we _____ the assignee.
   A. communicated with
   B. contacted
   C. telegraphed

2 Five days after the trial, a higher court _____ the jury's decision.
   A. ruled upon
   B. modified
   C. reversed

3 We must analyze these _____ to find out why they occur.
   A. explosions
   B. phenomena
   C. manifestations

4 We will reconsider your application when you begin a less hazardous _____ .
   A. activity
   B. pursuit
   C. occupation

5 The trainee _____ questions promptly and clearly.
   A. responded to
   B. answered
   C. reacted to

6 We will be glad to take care of the _____ for you.
   A. matter
   B. problem
   C. debt

7 They gathered _____ data on their field trip.
   A. accurate
   B. good
   C. excellent

8 Haggerty was able to _____ the furnace alone.
   A. operate
   B. stoke
   C. run

9 The men were divided into six _____ .
   A. categories
   B. crews
   C. groups

10 The profits from the three subsidiaries _____ $543,000,000
   A. were
   B. came to
   C. totaled

Below is a list of specific words and a letter containing many inappropriate general words, in italics. Substitute the specific words for the general words.

pamphlets	delivered
operation and construction	Field-Boy Lawn Mower
adjustable-height	rust
many years	repair
low	Field-Boy

Dear Sir:

Thank you for your interest in our *product*. Enclosed are two *items* describing its *characteristics* in detail.

You may be particularly interested in such features as the *movable* wheels, the aluminum body that will not *deteriorate*, and the carburetor that never requires *attention*.

We think you will get *a long period* of high performance from the *machine* for the *worthwhile* all-inclusive price of $120.50—*sent* to your home.

CHAPTER 6

The following ten sentences contain inflated language, wordy or unnecessary phrases, "the (noun) of" phrases, and wordy clauses.

1 We harvested in the neighborhood of 15,000 bushels of wheat this year.

2 Inasmuch as you want the withdrawal of your entire balance, the completion of Form 118-A by you is necessary.

3 He did it on the grounds that he needed money.

4 I must express my regret that Mr. George Colbert, who is our best public speaker, was not able to attend your meeting, which was held at the Peabody Auditorium.

5 It is my personal belief that this magazine should be published for people who own houses in the suburbs.

6 The decline of prices was the causative factor in my decision not to plant wheat last year.

7 We are looking forward with anticipation to meeting you at the earliest practicable date.

8 Although Mr. Barton's plan is of a controversial nature, it may help us in the finalization of the project ahead of schedule.

9 On the occasion of our last meeting, you asked several questions with reference to our personnel policy.

10 Mr. Nissley, who is the project's Chief Engineer, has approved the plans, which were recently revised.

CHAPTER 7

The following ten sentences are not clear either because the modifiers are misplaced or because they dangle. Revise them.

1   He wanted to finish the project badly.
2   He almost succeeds in anything he attempts.
3   The president said that he hoped all the salesmen would continue their hard-sell tactics at the board of directors meeting yesterday.
4   We recommend that you use a lighter motor oil in your car when it is hot and humid.
5   I persuaded him after he finished his consulting job to stay on with us as a permanent employee. (This has two interpretations. Give both.)
      A. _____
      B. _____
6   The customer had a large package talking to Mr. Bossone.
7   In two weeks, Professor Rice will conduct a seminar on techniques for constructing nuclear power stations in classroom B.
8   While trying to repair the computer, the lights went out.
9   After analyzing the samples, they were sent to the client.
10   Hoping to save precious time, your order was routed to the local warehouse.

CHAPTER 8

The following six examples lack subordination. That is, some of the ideas are expressed in forms that overemphasize their importance. Revise each example by reducing each undersubordinated idea to a clause, phrase, or single-word modifier.

1   Enclosed is an envelope that is convenient and self-addressed.
2   These new efficiency apartments have been designed for those who are in the professions.
3   The planning committee announced a new schedule for the production of tires for racing cars.
4   Mr. Pfiser is the area coordinator, and he will be glad to meet you on June 10.
5   The New York Stock Exchange provides a fair marketplace for common stocks. It does this also for preferred stocks. All these stocks include those of most of the major American corporations.
6   Enclosed is a copy of your manuscript, which has been edited and which is for your approval.

   The following sentence is oversubordinated. That is, it is made too long by too many modifying clauses and phrases. Break it up by making your editing changes right in the example.

7   A series of production mishaps on the X-2 Project put the Kessler firm two weeks behind schedule, leaving the way wide open for Chripac Computer Services to make a sales presentation of their sophisticated and expensive hardware to the project's sponsor, Armond-Hedges, Inc., known in the trade as an extremely schedule-minded client.

CHAPTER 9

Revise the following ten sentences so that there are no mistakes in parallelism.

1 Tying a knot is not difficult, but to splice a rope is another matter altogether.

2 You will receive instruction in writing computer programs and how to troubleshoot.

3 The scientist first states his hypothesis, then tests it, and then his conclusions are drawn.

4 Cleaning personnel should be careful to empty all ashtrays, to keep water carafes full, and closing all windows is advisable.

5 I have found that Mr. Albright is honest, reliable, and has a capacity for efficiency.

6 Your new assignment will include investigating the Aronson situation and to make out a full report for the senior vice president.

7 To state clearly all of a firm's major objectives is taking the first important step toward better management.

8 Speech lessons gave him confidence when speaking to a group or when he had to interview a job applicant.

9 We had hoped not only to increase sales last month but also the lowering of our inventory was to be effected.

10 We told the mechanic to check the dwell and timing and that replacement of the spark plugs should be accomplished.

CHAPTER 10

Match the link with the kind of relationship it announces to the reader.

Link		*Relationship*
1 And	A.	Here is another negative thought.
2 Or	B.	Here is an additional thought.
3 But	C.	Here comes a similar idea.
4 Nor	D.	Here is a supporting thought.
5 For	E.	Here is an alternative thought.
6 Moreover	F.	Here is a contrasting thought.
7 Consequently	G.	The next idea is the result of the previous
8 Therefore		idea.
9 Similarly	H.	The next idea follows logically from
10 Likewise		previous ideas.

Fill in an appropriate link in the following five sentences.

1 Many customers would like to buy this product, _____ I think we priced it too high.

2 Until early last year, the personnel department did not use aptitude tests when hiring and placing new employees. _____, employee turnover in the company was quite high.

3 Mr. Cramer gave an intelligent _____ entertaining speech on sales techniques he has found successful over the years.

4   The market for grapes in your area has not improved significantly, _____ will it until we change our distribution and sales system.
5   Sales for the past month have not been as large as we hoped. We are, _____, going to continue operating our factories at full capacity for at least another month.

CHAPTER 11

The following five sentences contain business jargon and inappropriate colloquialisms, slang, or clichés. Revise them so they become more natural.

1   It's been no bed of roses, here at the Southeastern sales office lately; in fact, new contract work has been as scarce as hen's teeth.
2   Not only does Mr. Johnson know all the "ins and outs" of the knitwear wholesale trade, but he is a crackajack financial analyst.
3   Permit me to express my grateful thanks for your latest order, which we will endeavor to fill by June 2.
4   If I may make so bold as to offer a suggestion, our Baby-Sitter Stroller shown on page fifteen of our catalogue may be of particular suitability for your needs.
5   Attached hereto please find our check in the amount of $586.27, which sum being the full payment of our account to date.

CHAPTER 12

The following six examples are negative and insulting. Revise them so that they become natural, friendly, and courteous.

1   If you do not mail your order by November 25, you will not receive this item in time for Christmas.
2   It is necessary that your payment in the amount of $20.61 be made to us no later than October 2.
3   The refund that I asked you for has arrived.
4   Your failure to achieve satisfactory results from your new dishwasher probably stems from erroneously using regular rather than hard-water detergents.
5   On weekdays, tickets cannot be purchased before twelve noon or after five P.M.
6   If you neglect to mail your employment application within three days, we will probably not be able to inform you of our decision before the end of the month.

CHAPTER 13

Make the following examples more *personal*.

1   As requested, I am enclosing a booklet describing our line of hi-fi equipment. It is hoped that something will be of interest. All orders will be promptly handled.
2   It is assured that we will meet the terms of our guarantee.
3   I'm always glad to receive a letter from one of our customers who is pleased with the Whirl-Jet Clothes Dryer.

4 This writer will be in New York during the week of April 26 and will be in contact by telephone to make an appointment.

5 After the medical examination has been made, the application forms should be returned to this office, and reinstatement of your life insurance policy will be considered.

CHAPTER 14

Below are three bad beginnings of three letters. Using whatever information is available, revise so that the *opening sentence* in each case meets the requirements you learned in the lesson. You do not have to revise the whole example.

1 This is ɔ inform you that we received your letter. In it, you made a collision-insurance clai·ɔ for $250. Enclosed is our check in payment of same.

2 Lately, we've been making quite a few changes in the way we handle our customers. You've probably noticed that your monthly checking-account statement has been redesigned. This letter is to help you read it.

3 I am glad to answer your letter of August 2. Here is the information you asked for.

Revise the following two endings:

4 The amount still owing on your account is $98.46. Your prompt attention to this matter will be very much appreciated.

5 If you have any more questions about our products, kindly do not hesitate to communicate with the undersigned.

Now solve the following writing problems:

6 You're the bookkeeper in the accounting department of a manufacturer of motorcycles. You receive a letter, dated January 28, from one of your best customers, the owner of a thriving dealership. He wants one of your invoices (bills) voided, and a new, corrected one sent. You check his files and have a new invoice typed up, so that you can include it with a letter. Write the opening sentence of that letter.

Dear Mr. Tolman:
_____

7 You're the manager of Acme Meats, Inc., a large wholesale meat supplier. Mr. Rodgers, who's just opened a steak house in your city, wants to buy his meat on credit. You decide to accept him as a credit customer because you've found his credit rating to be excellent. But he must first fill in and return the enclosed form. Write your opening and closing sentences.

Dear Mr. Rodgers:

A. (Opening sentence) _____
B. (Closing sentence) _____

8 A housewife has sent you a check for $22.95 to buy an Easy-ɔ .am Pressure Cooker, which your company advertised in a national magazine. Sın ⁄our company only sells through dealers, you are returning her check. You gıvɛ her the

address of her local dealer, Bediant's Appliance Store, and suggest that she go there to select the color she wants. Write the opening and closing sentences.

Dear Mrs. Connelly:

A. (Opening sentence) _____
B. (Closing sentence) _____

CHAPTER 15

Adjustment Letter

Here's the situation: You're the manager of a large photographic supply store in St. Louis. Monday morning, a box arrives. In it, you find an expensive camera and the following note:

Sherwood G. Briggs
118 State Street
Buffalo, New York 14202

October 16,

Peabody Photo Equipment, Inc.
52-81 Claxby Street
St. Louis, Missouri 63104

Dear Sirs:

Two months ago, when I was vacationing in St. Louis, I bought this Neverflex Camera at your store. But lately it hasn't worked right. Since it has a guarantee, I assume you'll repair it free of charge. Thank you.

Sincerely yours,

Sherwood G. Briggs

You take the camera to Mr. Porter in the Service Department and ask him to look at it. A few minutes later, Mr. Porter tells you that nothing is seriously wrong. The shutter mechanism must be replaced and the timing readjusted. He also says that it looks as if the camera was dropped or jarred in some way. You ask him how much it'll cost to repair it. He says $10.50.

You know that the guarantee covers "any defect of workmanship or materials within a year of normal use," but does not cover damage caused by accidents. So, before you can tell Mr. Porter to go ahead with repairs, you must get Mr. Briggs's agreement to pay the $10.50.

You will now write a letter explaining the situation. With the letter, you will enclose the following stamped, self-addressed postcard for Mr. Briggs to sign and return.

Yes, I agree to pay $10.50 for repair of my Neverflex Camera.

_____

(Please sign here.)

The purpose of this quiz is to see how well you include relevant ideas and exclude irrelevant ones. First, jot down the ideas you want to include. Don't worry about constructing sentences. (Make sure you deal with the main issue raised in Mr. Briggs's letter.) Then check to make sure you have sorted out all irrelevant ideas. Then write your letter.

CHAPTER 16

As the Training Director of a large city bank with over fifteen thousand employees, you receive the following letter of inquiry from an officer of a medium-sized bank in a nearby state.

Green State Bank
256 East Third Street
Salt Lake City, Utah 84118

May 10,

Mr. _____
Training Director
Seattle Bank
1506 Fourth Street
Seattle, Washington 98101

Dear Mr. _____ :

Several local manufacturing companies, which import a good deal of raw materials from abroad, have been coming to us more and more to help them with their foreign transactions, particularly with regard to letters of credit. While we welcome this new business, we find that we are a little over our head when it comes to foreign banking matters.

Our president, Mr. Leroy T. Slopes, was in your bank last month and talked briefly with Mr. Cable, head of your Foreign Banking Department. Mr. Cable mentioned that you will be giving a two-week seminar on the subject of letters of credit, starting next month

Would it be possible for one of our bright young men to attend? We would, of course, pay any fees or costs involved.

Sincerely yours,

James M. Seedtop
Vice President—Operations

You must refuse Mr. Seedtop for the following reasons, all or some of which you may want to mention in your turndown letter:

1 Your policy is to provide training and training materials to your own personnel only or to those in your correspondent banks. These are banks that have a special relationship with yours. That is, they maintain deposits at your bank, and in return, your bank performs services such as collecting their checks. (Mr. Seedtop will unde stand what you mean by the term "correspondent bank.") These banks, one of which is a local competitor of Mr. Seedtop's bank, have requested that the services of your training department be restricted, because they share costs with you to operate a cooperative training effort.
2 There is no more room in the upcoming seminar.
3 The seminar may be too advanced for Mr. Seedtop's bright young man.

You have made inquiries and have discovered that there are two training sources which may help Mr. Seedtop. One is a correspondence course called "The Basics of Foreign Banking," published by Goley and Tyson Publishers; the other is a five-volume programmed-instruction course called "Letters of Credit," put out by The American Bankers Association.

Now begin to think of what you will put in your refusal to Mr. Seedtop. What is your opening sentence going to be? Should the reasons for the refusal precede the actual refusal? How are you going to close? Can you do so on a positive note? Jot down your ideas. Then write your letter. Then rewrite it.

CHAPTER 17

Suppose you are a vice president in the Credit Department of the Tyco-Reemer Pipe Company, Inc., 1104 Kings Highway, Gary, Indiana 46401—a large manufacturer of steel, aluminum, and ceramic pipe and tubing. You have been reviewing financial statements and projections of the Arthur P. Knaur Construction Company, Inc., 311-12 West Third Street, Davenport, Iowa 52805, which has applied to your firm for an increase in its credit line from $20,000 to $250,000 in a letter dated May 15 from Mr. Harold L. Moon, Vice President. Knaur wants the increase because they have just won a million-dollar contract from Vally Electric, a local utility company to lay a 75-mile gas line. Thus, they estimate that they will need about $250,000 worth of 6" steel pipe.

You have been familiar with Knaur for several years and are confident that they have the experience and ability to complete such a project successfully. However, in going over their recent financial statements, you notice that the firm is already heavily in debt. In fact, total debt is about $500,000 while the net worth of the firm is only $600,000. Thus, if Tyco-Reemer Pipe sold Knaur $250,000 worth of pipe on credit, Knaur's total indebtedness would soar to $750,000—$150,000 more than the net worth. This would mean that Knaur's creditors would have more ...oney invested in the firm than its owners—a very unhealthy situation for a business in the construction industry, which needs to be financially in sound order to have the flexibility to meet unexpected contingencies. Thus, you must refuse to increase Knaur's credit line to $250,000.

In going over the contract between Knaur and the utility company, you note tnat it provides for a series of five progress payments of $200,000 each over the six months that the project is expected to last. You figure that if you allowed Knaur a credit line of $50,000 (i.e., they can purchase up to that amount of merchandise on credit), they could buy the pipe they need as they need it. That way, total debt would not jump to such an unhealthy level right away. Instead, the income from the progress payments would allow Knaur to keep debt down as it went along.

Now jot down the ideas you want to include in your letter to Mr. Moon, indicating your decision. Remember, you want to keep Knaur as a customer.

Then go over your list of ideas. Cross out any that are irrelevant. Which ones will you use in your opening? Your closing? Now write a draft of your letter to Mr. Moon and edit it to make it clear, concise, well organized, natural, courteous, and personal.

CHAPTER 18

Now you are required to write two letters—a sales letter and a collection letter.

The Sales Letter

You're the Sales Manager of Firefly Oil Company, Inc., 1377 Huron Street, Buffalo, New York 14202, a retailer of home heating oil. It's the middle of May, and you're sitting down to write a sales letter that will be included with this month's batch of bills to all customers. Your purpose is to tell them about Firefly's Special Spring Budget Plan.

This plan allows the customer to place his order for next winter's supply of oil (he must do so before June 15) and pay the amount of the order in three monthly installments over the summer. This has two advantages: (1) the lower spring prices, and (2) the peace of mind that comes from knowing that the whole winter's oil supply is paid for. Included is a self-addressed, stamped postcard giving the amount of oil that the customer purchased this past winter and its total cost and the same amount at spring prices. The customer has the choice of marking the "yes" or "no" box on the card, to show whether he wants the plan or not.

Read the above paragraphs several times. Jot down the ideas you want to include. Write your letter. Then revise it so that it is as persuasive as possible.

The Collection Letter

Now you are the Credit Manager of Firefly Oil. The firm's selling terms are 1 percent, fifteen days or net, thirty days. This means that your customers can take advantage of a 1 percent discount by paying within fifteen days of the monthly billing date or pay the full amount within thirty days.

It's the middle of May, and you're sitting down to write a collection letter to Dr. Donald K. Gilbert, 78 Stuyvesant Place, Buffalo, New York 14222, a physician and local homeowner—who has been a valued customer for five years and, until lately, has paid his heating bills promptly, always taking advantage of the discount. For some reason, he has not paid his last three bills, which now total $487.50. You have already sent him two polite reminders and have called his home several times but have not heard from him or been able to reach him. You have decided not to deliver any more oil until the present bill is cleaned up.

Now jot down what you are going to say to Dr. Gilbert. Are you to assume that all he needs is another "polite reminder?" What should the tone of your letter be? What arguments, if any, are you going to use to increase the likelihood of collection?

Once you have jotted down your ideas, write your letter and revise it.

INDEX

INDEX